Gonna Jump?... Take a Parachute!

Harnessing Your Power of Choice

Dave McSpadden

*How to make the rest of your life -
The best of your life!*

**Gonna Jump?...
Take A Parachute!**™
is a Copyright owned by the author and
RethinkAge Institute, LLC

The author's website:
http://RethinkAge.com

"*Gonna Jump?... Take A Parachute!: Harnessing Your Power of Choice*", Copyright 2011 by David F. McSpadden. Printed in the United States of America. No part of this book may be used or reproduced, in any manner whatsoever, without the written permission of the author, with the exception of brief quotations used in relationship with critical reviews and articles. For information please contact the author at Info@RethinkAge.com.

This book may be purchased in volume for use in educational, business, non-profit fund raising or promotional use.

For information on quantity discounts which qualify, please contact Info@RethinkAge.com.

FIRST EDITION
Cover Design: Susan Veach
Editor: Roger McManus
ISBN: 978-0-615-48898-1
EAN.UCC-13 - 978-0-615-48898-1
Library of Congress Control Number: 2011913095

© David F. McSpadden

What others have said:

"Dave McSpadden's first book - "Gonna Jump? Take A Parachute!"...FABULOUS. I hope he writes more books. It is a total toolbox for anyone who wants to perfect my dear friend Mark Victor Hansen's life goal: to 'make the rest of your life, the best of your life'. Interesting and information-packed, this book is a MAGNIFICENT collection of ideas and resources for some of the very best ways of being in transition and thriving."

Dr. John Dealey - *Author*, *International MasterMind Expert and Entrepreneur*

"Dave's book is upbeat and inspirational. A rather unique approach to addressing skills and qualities we all would benefit from improving in our lives. Read this book and Rethink Age!"

Elizabeth Lombardo, PhD - *Author of the bestselling book*, *A Happy You: Your Ultimate Prescription for Happiness*

"Many people go into retirement thinking about what they don't want (the job, the commute, the boss, the hassles) instead of thinking about what they do want. Dave's book helps people learn important lessons, make plans from those lessons, and "pull the rip cord" on their plans to make them a reality. Dave's analogy of the cords of life's parachute makes perfect sense for cultivating balance in all areas and most importantly, taking action by pulling the rip cord! An inspiring must-read for anyone considering a jump into a new phase of life!"

Lorrie Marrero - *Creator of ClutterDiet.com and Author of* *The Clutter Diet: The Skinny on Organizing Your Home and Taking Control of Your Life*

"*Gonna Jump* is the instruction manual that they should give all of us when we reach those big milestones in our lives: adulthood, college graduation, marriage, business launch, business sale, career transition, loss and retirement. It is at these times in our lives we need to remember that we did pack our parachutes and its time to check them and make sure we have accounted for all the cords. Each cord should be packed so we can use them in the moment they are needed for life's big and small jumps. Dave McSpadden is a superb jump master – easy to follow, a delight to learn from and someone whose advice you'd better remember when its your turn to leap."

Lorraine McGregor, CEO, Spirit West Management and MakeYourBusinessSaleable.com; *Author of Fast Track Secrets for Making Your Business Saleable*

"I have known and worked with David McSpadden for many years and consider him to be an outstanding visionary leader. Through David's excellent book, *Gonna Jump?...Take A Parachute!*, he provides all the tools one needs to make their vision a reality."

Bill Perryman, CPA, CFP

"In these 21st century times of increasing complexity, one thing is certain: our world will continue to evolve and change at exponential rates. Dave McSpadden has created an "operating manual" for baby boomers to guide us successfully through the changes – both internal and external – we face in negotiating the most challenging and potentially most rewarding third of our lives. Present moment awareness, mind-body-spirit alignment, and creativity are key to a working parachute, and Dave shows us how to pull the 'rip cord'."

John Dillon, *public radio host and author of* *The 20-20 Creativity Solution: Focus Your Natural Creativity for Success, Happiness and Peace of Mind*

"In today's unpredictable world, we all need a sturdy parachute to protect us and propel us forward so we can reach our chosen destinations quickly and safely. In *Gonna Jump*, Dave McSpadden shares his signature style of engaging humor and non-judgmental recommendations to enable us to create a dependable and dynamic parachute for life. Even the most stubborn of us will be moved to adopt McSpadden's well- researched strategies for maximizing potential in 9 critical areas of life. Why? Because Dave McSpadden is the Master of Longevity and he is impossible to ignore. You need only meet him once to know he lives his message. Read *Gonna Jump...* – get a copy for everyone you love – and then do what it tells you to do. You owe it to yourself and everyone who loves you to make sure that no matter what life sends your way, your parachute will be strong enough to sustain you."

Wendy Lipton - Dibner, M.A., *President of Professional Impact, Inc. and bestselling author of* Shatter Your Speed Limits™ – *Fast-Track Your Success and Get What You Truly Want in Business and in Life*

"Dave McSpadden was on top of the world: healthy, successful, approaching retirement.

And then his world turned upside down. But Dave had an internalized framework, a personal parachute that allowed him to land safely on his feet so he could rise to the top again. Fortunately for us, Dave's new book, "*Gonna Jump?... Take A Parachute!* shares his lifetime of wisdom and teaches us how to prepare not only for retirement, but for whatever we face as our next transition."

Mache Seibel, MD, *Author of*
*Eat To Defeat Menopause****, and***
Save Your Life: What to do in a Medical Emergency

Gonna Jump?...
Take A Parachute!

CONTENTS

Introduction		9
Chapter 1 -	"What.... Jump? I didn't plan to Jump!"	23
Chapter 2 -	Who Packed My Parachute?	35
Chapter 3 -	The Spiritual Cord	51
Chapter 4 -	The Mental Cord	67
Chapter 5 -	The Physical Cord	83
Chapter 6 -	The Vital Health Cord	105
Chapter 7 -	The Emotional Cord	127
Chapter 8 -	The Relationships Cord	151
Chapter 9 -	The Financial Cord	171
Chapter 10 -	The FUN Cord	189
Chapter 11 -	The Rip Cord	201
Acknowledgements		211
About the Author		215

INTRODUCTION

"The purpose of our lives is to give birth to the best that is within us."
- Marianne Williamson

For someone who always thought I was in control of my life it was like being in someone else's movie as I lay on a gurney in the emergency room wondering why the bright florescent light panels on the ceiling were so fuzzy.

Shortly after getting hooked up to various monitors, I heard the ER nurse say to some patient, "Yep, looks like you've had a stroke." My first reaction was "How could she be so rude to just pop off and say that to some poor frightened person?" Then I looked around the room to see who she was talking to. It was me! "What...me...stroke? This just isn't right!"

These were some of the thoughts racing through my mind on October 28, 2009. But, unreal as it seemed at that moment, several tests and brain scans later verified what the seasoned ER nurse seemed to know when she first saw me and copied down my symptoms – loss of eyesight in my left eye, reduced function of my left arm and leg, balance issues, slower responsiveness and somewhat fuzzy thinking.

Sure, I had a lot on my plate at the time. I was president and CEO of my own commercial construction company and, like so many others across the country, was struggling with the new economic realities of a recession as we entered our 26th year in business. This was just a mere 18 months after I, and our 30 employees, were celebrating our best year ever, with $44 million in revenues.

But, by the Fall of 2009, in addition to the economic downturn, we were also deeply embroiled in a fierce battle of litigation to collect the money owed to us on three hotel construction contracts that we had not only designed and built, but on which I had borrowed substantial sums of money to pay our bills and overhead. The attorney's fees to collect what was due to us was quickly gobbling up the rest of our cash so I had to begin to let my employees go. This was extremely difficult and painful for all of us.

While all of these challenges were going on in my business life, I was also serving as a Rotary International District Governor of 69 Rotary Clubs and over 3,000 Rotarians in a large area of North Central Texas. Among the many other duties of a District Governor, it is a requirement to visit with the board of directors of each club. These board meetings are then followed by the

Governor's official visit and speech and to the entire club.

Four months into my year of service, during my 39th club visit, I received my first clue that something was not quite right. As I looked across the board room table and listened to a report by Karen, the club president, I noticed many fuzzy objects floating up between us that were clouding the vision in my left eye.

Because there were so many people in the room, I chose not to acknowledge this "little distraction". But, when I rose at the end of the board meeting to make my way into the room where I was to speak, I noticed that my balance wasn't quite normal and found myself reaching out and feeling for the backs of chairs and door facings to steady myself as we made our way from one room to the next.

Making my way through the food line, I was thinking how grateful I was that I wasn't dropping my plate. Later, as someone was introducing me and just before my speech, I leaned over and whispered a request to my wife, Marilyn, to please keep an eye on me because something felt "out of sorts". I went ahead and gave the best motivational talk to the club members that I could muster under the circumstances. Throughout the talk I found myself uncharacteristically reaching for and leaning on the edge of the lectern (I normally love to walk around and not hug the lectern as a public speaker).

When my talk was over, as was customary, I received the thanks, congratulations, grateful comments, handshakes and even hugs from members of the club. For the first time ever, however, I had to do so from a seated position in a chair because it was so difficult to find my balance to stand.

In hindsight, I suppose that many stroke victims rationalize and deny what's happening to them the same way that I was in that moment. Marilyn was holding on to my arm as she helped me back to the car in the parking lot and drove me home.

During the hour-long drive home we discussed whether we should go to a hospital or just go on home. But, I speculated that I was just tired and so, comfortable with my self-diagnosis, I also self-prescribed that some rest was all that was needed.

That evening I was scheduled to meet with the board of directors of my own Rotary club, which was to be followed by a hospitality social at the home of one of our members. Not wanting to disappoint my fellow club members, Marilyn drove me to attend both events, but I found myself, again, having to sit down the entire time. We left early and I went to bed thinking that surely some rest would take care of everything.

The next morning, when I raised my razor to the left side of my face to shave, I was very surprised to watch as my razor disappeared in the mirror! Believe it or not, losing the vision in my left eye was the first time that I actually became alarmed. When I called my doctor's answering service and described what was happening to me, they said to have someone drive me to the Emergency Room immediately or call an ambulance.

As Marilyn drove me to the E.R., the only words that were exchanged between us were those that found agreement in the conclusion that we should have gone to the hospital the day before. So much for being smart enough to diagnose my own medical condition!

Fortunately, the cell damage was to the hippocampus area of my brain, which effects memory but did not create any major permanent loss of mobility or physical functions.

So, with three prescribed medications for lowering my blood pressure and managing cholesterol, and a short hospital stay later, I was back into my normal routine, although a bit slower and more cautious about my strength and balance.

I still had 30 more Rotary club visits to make before Christmas, had to run my company and meet with employees, subcontractors, suppliers and litigators. I was so extremely lucky to have been able to fully recover quickly. The knowledge that it could have had a much different outcome, and the "wake-up call" that it represents, was not wasted on me, as I will share with you later.

The cost of 14 months of litigation to collect on those defaulted contracts and a continued downward slide of the economy finally ended my quarter of a century-old company in May 2010. While definitely not the same as the death of a child, the death of the company, into which Marilyn, my employees and I breathed life and gave so much of ourselves over the years, was very painful.

I had always dreamed that someday I would sell my company to my employees or some other company that wanted to carry on my legacy of serving our clients by building beautiful and successful operating properties.

My vision of my own "exit strategy" had us taking the proceeds from such a sale and serving other people in the world, who I like to call our "Human Family". We would work part of the time on Rotary International projects around the world and use the balance enjoying our children and grandchildren for the rest of our lives.

But, God had a *better* plan.

MY JUMP!

The jump that I made was to dedicate myself to do something that I have been thinking about most of my adult life, but never felt I had the opportunity to do. Maybe it is common for each of us to harbor a secret desire to do something different while continuing to stay on the treadmill we create for ourselves by doing what we have always done.

In the year since making the inevitable decision to end my old company and start a new one, I have found my heart's passion in founding and launching the RethinkAge Institute. Today, as a professional public speaker, author, coach and seminar leader, I have the opportunity to serve and touch thousands and, maybe someday, millions of lives for the better. Helping teach, motivate and inspire our "Human Family" everywhere to find their passions, their higher purpose and to live their lives to the fullest, is an opportunity for which I am *very* grateful and want to share with all who will allow me to serve them.

I have taken a long and winding road to get here, but this is what will occupy my spirit, mind and body for the rest of my life. Had I not chosen to jump with the parachute that I had carefully created long before this significant transitional change, I would never have been able to share these principles with you and give you the opportunity to pass them on to others.

The good news is that I do have a parachute for this jump and I have learned how to steer it your way so that I can help you with the jumps and changes that are ahead of you in your life, whether that is contemplating retirement, a change of career, relocation to a new community or any other significant change event that lies ahead. At this moment, though, I need you to help me by visualizing this metaphorical parachute. The canopy is large, multi-colored and beautiful as it silently takes me to my favorite new destination of serving you, and my favorite new four-letter word. That word is NEXT!

The harness is snug and comforting in providing the support needed to see me through the winds of change as I bring my message to you. Very importantly, each of the main principles, which I call "cords", attached to my harness are the critically important elements that connect to the lift created by the canopy that buffers my journey and reduces the likelihood of crashes which would end my future flight. Each of these cords must be in balance and stay connected for the canopy to operate smoothly, securely and not flutter. Obviously, if one or more of the cords breaks, the canopy will not stay in tact and it's not going to be the ride I wanted, or of which I have dreamed.

Each of us has this same "parachute" available to us, whether we have thought about it or not. It exists to guide us through to secure and certain outcomes of the jumps (changes) that we face. When we do find ourselves either forced to jump, or jumping off into something new on purpose, how we have packed and use our parachute will largely determine the success of fulfilling our objectives.

Each cord of our parachute that is packed has a specific name and purpose. They are:

- The Spiritual Cord
- The Mental Fitness and Function Cord
- The Physical Fitness Cord
- The Vital Health Cord
- The Emotional Well-Being Cord
- The Relationships Cord
- The Financial Independence Cord
- The FUN Cord
- And, The Rip Cord

The last cord is critical of course. The metaphorical "Rip Cord" is that wonderfully comforting piece of woven fabric, attached to a "D" shaped metal ring that you pull to activate and unleash your parachute.

Whether you have ever actually parachuted from an aircraft or off of a high precipice on Earth, or not, it probably makes sense to you that *how* you use the rip cord is very important. Equally important is *when* to pull the rip cord since timing is significant to the outcome as well. Panic, and pull it too soon, and you may find yourself drifting on unseen winds to an unintended destination. Pull it too late, and, oh well – use your own expletive!

The inspiration to write this book comes from my desire to pay-forward my gratitude for the lessons that I have learned in my lifetime and the experiences accumulated from those lessons. A strong desire to honor those who have taught me is also part of my motivation. If by opening myself up and sharing what I have learned helps just one other person to live the life they always thought they were meant to live, and they then go on to share what they learn with others in our Human Family, the time and dedication it took to write this book was well invested.

This book was written in the spirit of a reference guide for how to *make the rest of your life the best of your life.* It is not intended to necessarily be read like a novel, from cover to cover sequentially. So, take your time, focus on the areas that interest you and, over time, take it all in at your convenience. Having said that, I will share that there is continuity between each of the "cords" of your parachute that deserve some thoughtful attention.

This book is not intended to be about me. It is only worthwhile if you choose to make it about you. So, let's make an agreement right up front; my part is that I will offer the best that I can in the way of knowledge, information and thought-provoking exercises for each cord of your parachute for you to consider. Your part is to not just read it but to find your own experience of it.

You can gain information by reading. But reading and thinking about something for a brief period is, by its very nature, *passive*. To truly make changes that will have a positive impact on your life you must translate that knowledge into your own experience. And, to experience something actually creates a potentially useful response in your brain that can translate into an *active* outcome.

The old adage that "knowledge is power" isn't necessarily true. But, I do believe *the use of knowledge* is power. So, I suggest that at the end of each chapter you capture the points that you want to translate into an active part of your life into your own personal journal. The following page is provided to you as a prompting format for capturing what you feel is the best way for you to summarize what you have gained – and want to apply.

Sample Journaling Framework:

POINTS I WANT TO REMEMBER AND EXPERIENCE:

1.

2.

3.

4.

5.

WHO ELSE COULD BENEFIT FROM WHAT I'VE LEARNED?

_____
_____
_____

It is in this spirit of partnership of a better future for you that I thank you for giving this book a read and for, hopefully, you consider how it can impact your life and those that you love and care about. Also, it is my hope, as you read it, you may discover one or more cords that need tuning up on your parachute.

As you journal your notes about how you might experience the benefits of tuning up your parachute cords, I ask that you share your experience of this book with others and, thus, make even more of a difference in your own journey. You can also share your outcomes and comments with me by visiting my website at <u>RethinkAge.com</u>.

Now, let's prepare for your NEXT big jump!

Webster's New World Dictionary defines the word "JUMP" as follows:

"**jump** (jump) *vi*, **1** to spring or leap from the ground, a height, etc. **2** to jerk; bob **3** to move or act eagerly: often with *at* **4** to pass suddenly, as to a new topic **5** to suddenly rise, as prices **6** (Slang) to be lively – *vt*. 1 *a)* to leap over *b)* to pass over **2** a distance jumped **3** to leap upon **4** to cause (prices, etc.) to rise **5** (Colloq.) *a)* to attack suddenly *b)* to react prematurely **6** (Slang) to leave suddenly [to jump town] – *n*. **1 a jumping** 2 a distance jumped **3** a sudden transition **4** a sudden rise, as in prices **5** a sudden, nervous start **get (**or **have)** the jump on [Slang] to get (or have) an advantage over......."

CHAPTER 1

WHAT...JUMP? I DIDN'T PLAN TO JUMP!

"The key is not to prioritize what is on the schedule, but to schedule your priorities."

- Stephen Covey

You may be wondering about the use of the word "jump" because you may think there is no jump in your future plans. But, stop and think about it. We live in a world that almost guarantees a change and transition. Sometimes a sudden transition is right around the corner for any one of us. Transitions in our lives come in many forms. A change of jobs or careers, loss of a loved one or friendship, starting a new business, divorce, moving to a different city or even the one called "retirement" are just a few of the jumps we can face in our future.

Within each of these events there is a jump from what was, to what will be. And, when any of these transitions occur, we are instantly presented with fresh opportunities to engage the most powerful gift we human beings possess, our God given *power of choice*.

Think about this for a moment. Human beings are the most blessed species on Earth. Our automatic possession of this gift of the power of choice is so amazing that we can even determine to end – or continue – our own existence. So, anything short of that known capability is also well within our ability.

In recent decades, it has seemingly become more and more popular for many of us to assume that we are mere *victims* of anything that is going on in our lives. It is estimated that over half of the members of the North American society believe most of what happens in their lives is not only beyond their control, they maintain the belief they are victims of _____ (fill in the blank: the government, the economy, their bosses, their co-workers, a sudden change in health, finances and on and on). Although most of what happens in your life may not be all that sudden, when the event arrives and the changes, consequences and pressure derived from those changes occur, it may make you *feel* like the impact is sudden in that moment of realization.

So, whether the jump happens as a result of something that you purposely planned and worked toward, or you feel it is something that "fell upon you," the message here is it doesn't matter. What matters is what you do with it, what you learn from it and how you apply it to your future to make your life, and the lives of those around you, better and more closely aligned with your best dreams and highest hopes.

A great example of this truth and one that most will face in the future – or may even be in the process of living with now – is the concept of retirement. The very decision to retire is one of the biggest and most dramatic "jumps" we can make. When I was 68, combining my almost insatiable appetite for studying human nature and my study of the change strategies of human psychology, I came to the realization that retirement, as it was originally intended, is not only much less relevant in our current times, it is not even necessarily a sound or healthy concept.

Ask yourself this question, "When I think about retirement, the first subject that comes to mind is _____?"

What is your answer? Is it money, travel, hobbies? Most of those whom I have had the chance to interview across North America will choose one of these three answers as their first response. Predominantly their answer is about money. In developed, and frankly privileged, countries this is not only the first answer, it has become a cultural norm. The thought seems to be, "If I have enough money when I retire, everything else will work out". This could not be further from the truth.

Have you ever heard of someone who retired and within a few years they became ill and died? Of course you have! And, this occurs regardless of how much money they had. Is this an urban myth? Well, I encourage you not take my word for it. Get online and do your own research for the truth about the, often devastating, effects of the choices many people are making around the concept of retirement.

There are many retirees who are self-medicating with alcohol or prescription drugs, like antidepressants, who are slowly digging themselves into a spiritual, mental, physical, emotional and financial hole out of which they will find it increasingly difficult to overcome. Personally, I respect the old saying about such holes which says, "If you see you're digging one, you'd better quit. There is no future in it!"

Obviously, there are also many who are quite happy in their retirement. However, I would even challenge those folks to search deeply within themselves and take a gut inventory-check to see if they feel they are thriving in all areas of their lives. By "all areas", I mean that we humans have the ability to achieve peak performance in the spiritual, mental, physical fitness, vital health, emotional, financial, relationships and FUN areas of our lives on a daily basis.

How would you rate your performance and feelings in each of these areas? Seriously, on a scale of 1 to 10 (with 1 representing non-existent and 10 representing outstanding) take a moment and determine how you feel you are doing right now in:

Spiritual Well-being _____

Mental Fitness and Function _____

Physical Fitness _____

Vital Health _____

Emotional Well-Being _____

Financial Independence _____

Relationships _____

FUN _____

Whatever your answers, you have just begun to create your Motivational Action Plan (MAP) that can lead you to the most high-performing, fulfilling, compelling and extraordinary times of your life. *It is within you to create the changes you want to become and experience.* From this list of your most honest answers and considerations come the choices of where you *do* want to jump into your future with full faith in the outcome and a child-like wonder of it all!

This process will require you to engage all of the areas that you just rated for yourself. It is about your choices concerning the concept of retirement. By exploring this area of your life, you will hopefully start an important conversation about the concept of retirement within your family and your circle of friends.

To begin with, it is important to understand where the whole concept of retirement originated. So let's look at the history of the concept of retirement as described by **Wikipedia** - the (online) free encyclopedia:

> *"**Retirement** is the point where a person stops employment completely. A person may also semi-retire by reducing work hours.*
>
> *Many people choose to retire when they are eligible for private or public pension benefits, although some are forced to retire when physical conditions don't allow the person to work any more (by illness or accident) or as a result of legislation concerning their position. In most countries, the idea of retirement is of recent origin, being introduced during the 19th and 20th centuries. Previously, low life expectancy and the absence of pension arrangements meant that most workers continued to work until death. Germany was the first country to introduce retirement in the 1880s.*
>
> *Nowadays most developed countries have systems to provide pensions on retirement in old age, which may be sponsored by employers and/or the State.*

> *In many poorer countries, support for the old is still mainly provided through the family. Today, retirement with a pension is considered a right of the worker in many societies, and hard ideological, social, cultural and political battles have been fought over whether this is a right. In many western countries this right is mentioned in national constitutions."*

I hope you caught some of the important trigger points in this definition. First, "many people choose to retire when they are eligible for private or public pension benefits". Money is the decision trigger, not the better question of "Am I spiritually, physically, mentally and emotionally ready to make major changes in my sense of purpose, meaning, contribution and belonging?"

Second, that "Germany was the first country to introduce retirement in the 1880's." Guess what triggered that event, even then? Yep, you guessed it – Money! It seems that Chancellor Otto Von Bismarck and his advisors became concerned over a growing unrest among their working class citizens and the working class perception of the lack of caring by the ruling government. To quell the unrest caused during the "workers' movement", an insurance (pension) scheme was devised whereby anyone who reached 65 years of age would receive a government "pension" designed to allow them to discontinue working and enjoy "old age". But there was a catch! Here is how Wikipedia briefly describes the program:

Old Age and Disability Insurance Bill of 1889

The Old Age Pension program, financed by a tax on workers, was designed to provide a pension annuity for workers who reached the age of 65 years. At the time, the life expectancy for the average Prussian was 45 years.

You can't help but notice that the chances of the government paying back any of the money that they gathered through taxes, along with some promised Federal Government money to fund this scheme, were most likely safe from ever being put into use given the trigger age of 65 for receiving the payments and the average life expectancy being age 45. Although "life expectancy" was influenced by a high mortality rate among children of that era, Chancellor Von Bismarck and his advisors certainly had designed a reason to feel that the Federal Government treasury was safe under this plan while they benefitted from the public relations aspect of this concept.

By 1911, Great Britain and other European countries had adopted similar plans, with similar parameters. Then, in 1935, U.S. President Franklin D. Roosevelt managed to copy the "European Model" and convinced the Congress to pass the "Old Age Survivors, and Disability

Insurance" program, better known as the *Social Security Act of 1935.*

President Roosevelt's "New Deal" programs were primarily focused upon government-funded public works projects to "create jobs" and pull the U.S. out of the Great Depression of the 1930's. But, the emphasis on the "Old Age" legislation was to stimulate and encourage the "old" people (age 65 in the original Act) in the workforce to step aside and help create jobs for younger workers. This stigma of creating the belief that "old" people should get out of the way for younger people is still culturally prevalent today. The problem is that the original intent of the Act is simply not relevant today.

First, even the current eligible retirement age of 62, from my humble perspective, is no longer relevant as an automatic marker for what is "old". Second, the average life expectancy in 1935 had not reached 62. So, again, the government's bet on long term payouts were seen as a safe one (for the government, not for the proposed recipients). Third, the current population of the Baby Boomer generation, people born from 1946 to 1964, is approximately 76.5 million!

I believe all nations need this generation for their experience, their wisdom, their innovations and entrepreneurial spirit to contribute to the economy, not to just sit down over the next 18 to 40+ years of their lives. This I know for certain - *if you sit down, chances are you will shut down. Period!*

If you haven't yet drawn the conclusion about my perspective on retirement, I want to say it loud and clear: one of the underlying purposes of this book is to start you thinking about the benefits of "flunking" retirement successfully (at least in the traditional definition of the term) either now, or whenever in the future the decision to retire becomes relevant for you.

We humans were not wired to be inactive. Starting in 2011, and for the 18 years that follow, Baby Boomers are hitting the "retirement age" around the world at a rate never before seen. This, alone, should spark some conversation about how you can rethink retirement and how you can begin planning your life now for when you enter your 50's, 60's, 70's, 80's, 90's and beyond, so that the rest of your life *is* the very best of your life.

Aging is not the problem. We will all keep aging, at least chronologically, if we're lucky. The alternative to aging is final and permanent. But "growing old"? That is a *choice*!

I am sure you know someone younger than you who thinks, acts and talks like a person much older than you are. If this is someone to whom you are close, it is painful to watch them choose to behave this way. You recognize the symptoms in their attitude, their weight gain, their unhappiness and their lack of energy, ambition or their lack of a compelling vision for the future.

Hopefully, you also know someone who is much older than you but is full of energy and life. They are not just surviving, they are *thriving*!

So, which will you choose? Again, it is a choice. How wonderful it is that this choice is available to each of us!

If you are thinking, "Now hold on, Dave. I have *this* problem, or, *that* issue, or, you just don't know the challenges that I face. How can you tell me that I have a choice?"

When those sorts of thoughts begin to occupy your mind, that is *exactly* when you need to check in on what it is you *do* believe to be true about yourself.   Do you believe you are the victim, or the victor?

Andre Godin once wrote - *"The quality of your expectations will determine the quality of your actions."*

I would add the quality of your actions and attitude will then largely determine the quality of your outcomes. One of my friends and mentors is a peak performance coach named Jeff.

Jeff represented the USA as an Olympic cyclist in 1972. Now Jeff runs a wellness center and is a chiropractic practitioner, speaker and peak performance coach for executives, entrepreneurs, performing artists and professional athletes.

You may never see yourself as a competitive Olympic or world-class athlete. But, a mountain of learning can be applied to anything you want to achieve in life that does come from the peak performance attitude of an Olympic athlete.

We will cover even more about Jeff and his message for you in the chapters that follow, but, for now just know this message from Jeff, "*No one ever stepped up on the podium to receive their Olympic medal that didn't see themselves there first!*"

That is also what the quote by Andre Godin expresses perfectly. And yes, as a member of our human species, you have it within you to *see* yourself on whatever "podium" of accomplishment that you want to conceive, believe in and achieve! The only way you will not, is to decide in the beginning, or as the challenges increase, that your excuses are more important and carry more weight than the outcome you envision achieving.

Everyone knows there will be jumps of change in the future for all of us. But, more importantly, I would like you to harness up your own parachute that will help ensure you arrive safely, and with a greater degree of certainty, at the destination you visualize for your life's journey.

Also, I want you to develop the confidence to leave your comfort zone and jump when opportunities present themselves to you. The confidence that I am writing about comes from knowing that the large, beautiful canopy of your parachute is supporting you on your journey through a crystal blue sky. It is connected with strong, balanced and dependably reusable cords that you have chosen to create to put you in greater control on the path to your future joy and fulfillment.

That's where we are going NEXT!

CHAPTER 2
WHO PACKED MY PARACHUTE?

"Skill to do comes of doing."
- Ralph Waldo Emerson

Please bear with me as I go into some detail about the history and development of the parachute with some related illustrations. My purpose is to get us both thinking within a similar space to be able to use the parachute as a powerful metaphor throughout this book.

The parachute is a most interesting and, for most of us, scary apparatus. The invention was developed in the 15th century (Figure 1) as both a means of attempting human flight and also as a possible method to survive the vagaries of early hot air balloon flights.

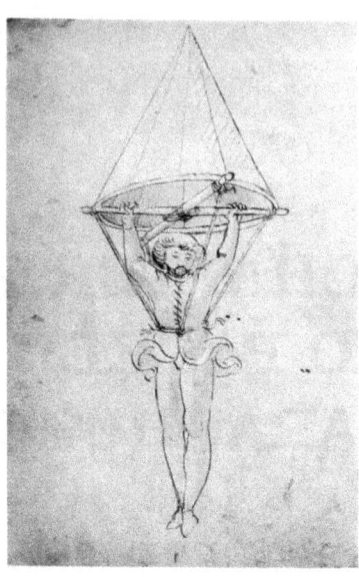

Fig. 1 - The oldest known depiction of a parachute, by an anonymous author (Italy, 1470s)

The word parachute is a made up from two French words - *para* which means "to protect against"; and *chute* which means "fall". As you can imagine, most of the earliest attempts were not successful and had dire consequences for the experimenters. The most common contemporary vision of parachutes comes from paratroopers going into battle by launching themselves from an aircraft to their desired strategic destinations (Figure 2). Since original round parachutes were designed to primarily induce drag and slow the terminal velocity of descent, actual guidance to a desired destination was crude and problematic at best in the earliest days for military paratroopers.

Fig. 2 - Round parachutes opening for U.S. Army Paratroopers

I am sure that you can easily picture in your mind the parts of the more modern parachute. A simple description of its parts are the canopy, which connects to the cords, which then connect to a harness attached to the person or payload. For many years all of this connected apparatus was activated or released by pulling on the rip cord. You can visualize the rip cord as having a "D" shaped metal ring for the parachutist to grab hold of and pull to unleash all of the pins that hold the cords and chute within the pack.

As in all such devices, the technological and testing advances have not only improved the design and usefulness of the parachute, but it has also morphed into a device that also provides some degree of forward motion and control so that the modern "square" or "ram-air" parachutes are airfoils that fly like a wing. So, after over 500 years of development, they can actually achieve the forward flight that was dreamed of by the original inventors.

A great illustration of a square, ram-air parachute is shown in this photo (Figure 3). That's me making my first tandem parachute jump hanging out in front of my jump-master, Kevin.

Photo by Marilyn McSpadden

Fig. 3 - Example of a square, ram-air parachute with the Author in a tandem jump.

Imagine that each of the areas of your life, that you rated in the previous chapter, are the "cords" of the modern parachute in your life that connects you to your own ram-air canopy. Your maneuverable square canopy and the cords that you use for connection and guidance, will not only protect you against a fall, but will also provide you a controllable forward motion to take you where you wish to go in the future. Obviously, if this is your device for safety *and* destination, you might want to consider who is packing your parachute, right?

In whose hands are you placing your life's future?

As a licensed single engine pilot, I subscribe to the old pilot mantra and I have never had the urge to "actually jump out of a perfectly good airplane." However, I have friends who have gone "skydiving", as they call it, and when I listened to their stories of the joy of overcoming their fears and experiencing the "sport", I found myself interested in giving it a try.

This is because I began to realize that, beyond the old pilot mantra, I had developed a genuine fear about jumping that I didn't want to carry around with me any longer. So now I have had the opportunity to experience my first parachute jump, as you saw in Figure 3. It was amazing and I will use the knowledge I gained from this experience for my metaphorical purposes in this book. You can also watch the video of this flight at RethinkAge.com

In the military, professionally trained "riggers" pack all of the parachutes. But, I was surprised to learn it is not that way in the private citizen world of skydiving, or sport parachuting. Although the safety (or reserve) chute is always packed and regularly inspected by a licensed rigger, frequent skydivers pack their own main chutes!

After internalizing that concept, it dawned on me; that's just like our lives! We are each responsible and accountable for our main outcomes on a day-to-day basis. But, when we want to seek additional reserve help to get through an unexpected circumstance, it is comforting to know that there are licensed professionals to help protect us with our "safety chutes" on just about any subject imaginable.

When developing the parachute analogies, I did some research on my own, as well as incorporating the stories of friends who *do* jump out of airplanes on a frequent basis. One friend in particular, by the name of Bill Dendy, has helped me find the flavor and feelings for parachuting. Bill has completed hundreds of jumps and absolutely loves to talk about them. I consulted with him as I prepared to write this book so that my analogies would be at least accurate enough to be credible. Bill is one of those people who, when he tells stories about something that he truly loves, makes you almost feel like you are right there. You feel as if you are experiencing each moment and each emotion so much that, in this case, you can almost sense the wind in your face.

Although I am using nine cords for the purpose of my analogies in this book (including the Rip Cord), Bill has taught me about the many cords of a "real" parachute. From each main cord, there are other cords branching out to provide more precise control of the modern square parachute. However, in using the "cord areas of your life" analogies in the following chapters, we will call the cords that connect us directly to our harness the "main cords".

Bill has had hundreds of jumps with only a couple of incidents. The few times that he has had the unexpected happen, it has been a combination of training, practice, skills, good luck and God's Will that he is still here to share it today. On both his 50th and his 300th jump his cords came out of the pack in a knot and he had to go to alternate solutions. There are various names for this failed type of knot (I suppose the names also coincide with the first words that pop into one's head in such a moment). I will spare you the names here.

The first time it happened, he panicked and cut the main assembly loose and went immediately to his reserve chute at a higher than normal altitude. With this early deployment, he ended up far from his destination.

On his 300th jump, his experience and skill kicked in and he managed to think through and determine that he had just enough time to hand reel the knot close enough that he could unravel it and let the main chute fly him to his intended destination.

In both incidents, only a few precious seconds passed between recognizing the problem and acting on a solution. As scary as that sounds, the two events represent a great metaphor for many experiences in our lives.

If asked, you could probably come up with a time when you realized that you had developed a "knot in your cords" and your "parachute" was spinning uselessly as you felt the sensation of falling. The first few times this occurred, you may not have had enough experience or maturity to know how to overcome the dilemma. But, as you gained experience with your "jumps", you became a more accomplished and, possibly, a master problem-solver.

While professional riggers are put through rigorous training and certifications before earning their license, there is still the fact that you are putting your life in the hands of another human. I wonder, does the phrase "human error" ever sneak into the mind of a skydiver?

How can you pack your parachute with complete confidence? Know that you have done your homework? Paid attention to the little "gotcha" type of details? How can you prepare yourself enough to know, for *certain*, you can make a committed decision to *take action* with total faith in the outcome?

This is where we really start to compare the sport of parachuting to your future life.

Many years ago, in his bestselling book, *Awaken The Giant Within*, Tony Robbins wrote, *"Your life changes the moment you make a **new, congruent** and **committed** decision."* Few statements have proven to be truer in my life. This *is* packing your parachute!

Of course, to experience the achievement of your vision, you must still jump and, oh yeah, *open the chute* at some point. But, making that initial decision, using your power of choice to jump (risk change), is the beginning action that makes all else possible.

The wonderful reminder is that each of us is already in possession of this power. The key ingredient to add, then, is an unalterable commitment of personal accountability for the outcome.

Exposure to my most powerful and moving example of personal accountability came in 1995 from my friendship with a very special man by the name of Hugh Bradley. The day I met Hugh was the day he came to our Rotary Club as the program speaker. That day changed my perspective on personal accountability. The way I was raised, I always believed we should each be accountable for what we choose to think, say and do. But Hugh raised the bar for me on just what personal accountability truly means.

Hugh rolled himself to the lectern in a battery powered wheelchair like no one in the room of

80+ Rotarians had ever seen before. You see, Hugh was a quadriplegic and had no use of his arms, hands, legs or feet. The air tube that was propped up to the vicinity of his mouth allowed Hugh to send short bursts of air to signal various commands to his wheelchair. Using this technique, he put the entire audience in awe as his wheelchair seat began to rise and place him into a near standing position at the microphone. We almost wanted to applaud him just for this first silent maneuver that placed him squarely into position, just like any other speaker would be.

Then Hugh began to speak. First, his words focused very briefly on his condition, what he perceived as some limitations and his magical machine but, then he quickly dove into his real purpose for coming to our club.

He told us of a small town in Mexico that he had "adopted" and that, over a period of years, and many trips, he and his driver had made the long journey in his van to that village to teach the residents there about building all types of buildings using concrete work, carpentry, electrical systems and roofing. He simply asked for any one of us who thought we might be able to assist him in his work to visit with him after the meeting because, he said, "When you take on the needs of an entire village, you can use any sort of help you can get!" I was having one of those moments – you know the kind, when I felt like he was talking directly to me, and that I must respond in some way.

When the meeting ended, I waited my turn as so many of our members met him individually and complimented him on both his talk and his mission work. Then it was my turn. I couldn't wait to tell him that over the many years of my construction business career I had accumulated a stockpile of various tools that I wanted to donate for him to deliver to the people that were the object of his cause.

He recited his address which was in a community just about 20 minutes away from where I lived. He also gave me his phone number and said I should call before dropping by with the tools. Of course, I agreed.

When I did call to tell him I was all loaded and ready to come, I was surprised to hear Hugh actually answer the phone. "How does a man answer the phone without the use of his arms?" I asked myself. His cheerful voice over the phone and inviting manner made me feel that I couldn't get there fast enough.

As I knocked on the front door of his house, I heard his voice from somewhere in the back and to the left of the entrance of his home as he said, "If that's you, Dave, come on in and turn left to come to my room down the hall".

I entered the small one-story home and did as he directed. At the end of the hallway was Hugh's combination bedroom, office and "mission central" headquarters. Hugh was lying on a hospital-type bed with some type of "headset" looking apparatus on his head. An "erector set-like" contraption was built over his bed that held a computer monitor with the screen looking down on him and his ever-present air tube at his mouth. I was in awe!

He welcomed me as if I was his long-lost brother and asked me to sit down. He then began to explain all the things he could do with what I was observing as an inventor's laboratory of gadgets. He explained that he had created a non-profit mission and was sending out newsletters and written requests for donations to support his charitable work for those villagers who were in need.

I asked him who was typing his newsletters and solicitations for help (this was before email). That is when he demonstrated the contraption on his head. It was a laser pointer that aimed a laser beam to a point on the computer monitor above his bed. With small movements of his head he could aim the beam to the letters on the image of a keyboard on the screen. He aligned the beam onto the "key" on the picture of a keyboard on his monitor. Once located, he would then send a small burst of air into his ever-present air tube and the computer would type that single letter. Hugh smiled as he said, "This gives a whole new meaning to the term 'hunt and peck' typing."

We both shared a chuckle, but again, I was amazed that this man was running his self-proclaimed missionary movement by searching for and "typing" one air burst letter at a time. He could also answer the phone, send messages, collect donations, map out his travel plans, organize speaking engagements and, essentially, run an entire missionary campaign with his own willpower. Of course, he also had the help of these ingenious inventions, his driver and his wife, Pat. Remember, this was before the Internet and emails and all the other "smart" devices that are available today.

I did a quick check to make sure that my mouth wasn't hanging open, cleared my throat, pushed back a tear and mustered my courage to ask *the* question. "Hugh", I asked, "how did this happen to you?" He only paused for a moment before rolling his face partially toward me and began to tell me his story.

At the age of 24, he was driving all night across New Mexico. Since I have been there and know how straight, flat and somewhat boring the drive can be, I acknowledged the image of the scene with him. He said that he was driving alone and fell asleep at a high rate of speed. He couldn't describe the accident because he didn't remember much about it, he said.

The first thing he said he remembered was being awakened by the painful cries of a man in the room with him. He woke up with the first thoughts of, "why doesn't someone see to this man and help him stop screaming?"

Hugh went on to reveal that, since no one seemed to be coming, he decided to roll over and see if he could determine what was going on and see if he could help the guy. When he tried to roll, he suddenly fell off the stainless steel table and hit the tile floor. No matter what injuries that he had suffered up to that moment, his impact on the floor now added a broken neck to the list.

In this same moment he also realized that the screams that had awakened him were his own. As he moved his eyes about, he discovered he was in this room all by himself. He didn't know if this was a treatment room or what, but he did know that, in that moment, he was utterly alone.

He went on to say that he somehow knew that since he survived, their must be more for him to do. "That", he said, "was over twenty years ago." Then, with no bitterness or victim tones in his voice, he calmly told me he had been finding his way to his purpose on this earth ever since.

I could not hold back my tears as the emotions washed over me. What an amazing human! What would I have done under the same circumstances? How did Hugh find the faith and the courage to dedicate his life to serving others? He touched my heart in a way that few have and I was forever transformed by his inspirational example of what personal accountability really means.

Hugh is no longer with us, but, his spirit lives on in all of the lives he touched, including mine. Sharing this story is just one more small way that I can honor him and let his inspirational life touch yours.

Hopefully, by now, you are asking yourself this compelling question, "If Hugh Bradley can start with nothing as a quadriplegic and built a lasting legacy, what can and will *I* do?" Hugh jumped into his future by packing his own parachute and finding his purpose along the way.

By his example, I ask you to understand when I tell you without hesitation, no matter your personal circumstances, you have it within you to determine your destiny. You can find your passionate purpose and to pack your parachute with the knowledge and confidence that, on your inevitable jump to what's next, you can succeed, you can contribute and you can make a difference! You are important, unique *and you matter* to the rest of your Human Family!

NEXT it's time to start packing your parachute!

CHAPTER 3
THE SPIRITUAL CORD

"The miracle is this – the more we share, the more we have."

- Leonard Nimoy

"You should never discuss politics or religion." Have you ever heard that warning? Growing up I heard this one a lot. But, I always wondered, "Why not?" If there were two subjects that are important enough to be the object of a healthy exchange of thoughts, beliefs and ideals, because of the enormous impact they have on our lives, it would be these two, right?

I suppose the admonishment was created for those who were as concerned about being on the receiving end of the judgment of others as much as it was a rule of thumb about what constitutes "politically correct" conversation. While

I do believe that both subjects need more investigation, exchange, understanding and tolerance, this chapter is not about either subject – politics or religion.

I can separate spirituality from the practice of religion and it is my hope you can also. I invite you to join me in this chapter with the understanding that nothing presented here represents my judgment or reflection about the values, beliefs or rituals of any particular religion. Instead, I want us to explore some basic principles – in fact, what I believe to be *Universal Laws* – that I have lived by, with worthwhile results for those whom I have served and for me, personally.

It is amazing to me how few people I meet who have a true understanding of what a blessed and uniquely amazing species we human beings are. As Marilyn and I have traveled different parts of the world, whether in North or Latin America, Africa, Europe or the South Pacific and met people in each of those locations, we are continually reminded of how much we humans are alike, regardless of where we were born, how we were raised or what our socio-economic background may have been. And, even from a spiritual point of view, most people in the world seem to be seeking the same thing. In fact, there seems to be a constant throughout all human cultures and across historical timelines that the condition of being human contains within it a common denominator. That common denominator is seeking *fulfillment*, here and in the hereafter.

No matter what variations of beliefs exist amongst the billions of people on the planet, the vast majority of Earth's inhabitants realize, at least somewhere within their inner being, that we are all connected and endowed by our Creator to seek our path toward fulfillment. Most spiritual teachings throughout history have indicated, if not said outright, that we are God's creatures, created in *His* image.

In the spiritual teachings of the Eastern faiths, there is also the belief that we are all part of the same Creative Energy of the Universe. Each of us is a sacred being who carries within us a connection to the Creator. Also, we are the creatures who, in physical form, can manifest our Creator's influence in the world by finding ways for each of us to best serve our Human Family and our planet.

If you were raised in any particular religious faith, it was probably common for you to be encouraged to live a more "God-like" life; again, referring to the choices you faced on a daily basis. As such, we each have the spiritual opportunity, and even the responsibility, to make our journey on this mortal plane one that makes a difference – a legacy – so we can also contribute to our own fulfillment and the fulfillment of others.

You have to know, even though you may not want to focus on it, that none of us is going to get out of this mortal plane alive. When our time on this Earth is finished, no matter what you believe about an afterlife, it is the end of our lives here. Period. What doesn't end, for sure, is the legacy that you leave behind through your gifts of influence to others. Much of how you influence others, throughout your life, depends upon both your shared philosophy and your behavior.

There is a relationship between psychology and spirituality. Your behavior and personality are an outward expression of your inner attitude. Your attitude is dictated by what you believe to be true about yourself and about others. These beliefs are manifested from the dominating *habits* of thought that occupy your mind. Those dominating habits of thought have their roots in everything you were taught and raised to believe since birth.

Obviously, you had no choice about most things early in your life. Parents, family members, siblings, members of your religious faith (if, like me, you were raised in a religious faith), teachers, friends and the media all had enormous influence on the dominating thoughts that occupied your mind as you made the journey from infancy to adulthood. Now that you are an adult, who chooses your thoughts?

Seriously, who is responsible for choosing your thoughts moment-to-moment, day-by-day and year-in and year-out from this day forward? Of course – *you are!* You have to pack your own cords of your parachute. The result becomes your desires for what you want to fulfill in your life on your own path to fulfillment. In other words, these are your motives for action (motiv/action), more commonly referred to as your *motivation*. What motivates you to make the choices of the thoughts that dominate your mind? From a spiritual perspective, *this* is worthy of your own self-examination.

Regardless of where you fall in your own very personal and private beliefs, when each of us reaches the end of our lives, we would like to know, for certain, that our being here has made a difference.

My friend Brendon Burchard, a very successful speaker, author, seminar leader, online marketer and founder of Experts Academy, has a tag line he uses to close every seminar, recording or communication that he produces. This tag line was created from his own near-death experience. It is posed in the form of three questions that are run into one overall guide to each and everyone of us, as well as of himself. The tag line is, "Did I really live? Did I really love? Did I really matter?"

I have heard him use this expression many times and each time I hear him ask it, especially with the sincere tone in which he asks, I know there is a deep spiritual component to his question. I would like for you to consider these questions for yourself, since the answers you will discover will surely reveal yet another path to fulfillment and spiritual enlightenment. And, again, you already possess the power to ask, and answer, these questions in every moment of your life!

The Spiritual Marriage of Intention-and-Attention

Dr. Wayne W. Dyer is an internationally renowned author and speaker in the field of self-development. In his best selling book, *The Power of Intention*, Dr. Dyer's research has concluded that intention is *"a force in the universe that allows the act of creation to take place."*

In his book he states that *"intention is not something you do, but is an energy that you are both a part of and a field of energy you can access to begin co-creating your life!"* He writes that life is a constant, eternal process that is always purposeful. In fact, Dr. Dyer says *"....there are no accidents and each of us was intended to be here, precisely on purpose as that is the only way Intention ever does anything."*

Dr. Dyer suggests if you don't like the way your life is right now, you must take notice and then take responsibility for your part in the creation of it. You must quit complaining about what doesn't work for you or what you don't like about your life and, instead, choose your thoughts based on what you *want* in your life. The creative energy that forms life works absolutely perfectly for everyone all of the time and it can only bring you what you think about and ask to be manifested in your life.

It takes discipline to continuously use your God-given power of choice to bring about a progressive realization of spiritual fulfillment for any of us. One of the best examples of discipline we have in the new millennium lies within the story of Tiger Woods. At his peak Tiger was considered the most dominant golfer of the game. There were many professional golfers who were physically larger, possibly stronger and had more years experience than Tiger did through the most dominant years of his professional career. So to what did he credit much of his success? Most of us know the story of how Tiger watched his dad swing a golf club in their garage while still an infant.

What you may not know, however, is that Tiger's mother was a very spiritual practitioner as a Buddhist. Once, in an interview for television, he stated that early in life she taught Tiger that if you want to achieve enlightenment, you have to do it through meditation, present-moment awareness and self-improvement through the mind. "That's something she passed on to me; to be able to stay calm and use my mind as my main asset."

The benefit of being in a present moment awareness, which can also occur during prayer, is something I learned from my parents. So it is certainly not exclusive to Eastern spirituality. My parents have practiced a lifetime ritual of setting aside a quiet period every morning at breakfast to share a Devotional reading, pray and connect to their present-moment awareness of the role their spirituality plays in both their lives and the lives of others.

There is a huge difference between being in present-moment awareness and just "thinking."

A great example of this can be seen in the game of golf. Even less skilled golfers like me know that, no matter how many hours we may have invested on the driving range, when we are out on the course and that little ball is just sitting there, not even moving, and we have a club in our hands, our minds are either our greatest ally or our biggest enemy. Why is that?

This one word, *thinking*, is worthy of examining for all of the other areas of our lives, including our spirituality. Continuing the analogy, often a golf instructor who is attempting to match a golfer's performance with their potential will ask, "When you were swinging the club just then, what were you thinking?"

The less-skilled golfer will easily recall a long list of thoughts that were racing through his or her mind like; keep your head down, control the backswing, keep your eye on the ball, distribute your weight, attain proper grip, follow through, and the list goes on.

When the same golf instructor asks the skilled golfer, "When you were swinging the club just then, what were you thinking?" The most common answer is **"*nothing*"**. Those golfers with the greatest skill focus on being present, in that one critical moment, and trusts the guiding power of the spirit, the mind and the well-practiced body to just "let go" to that trust.

Many athletes, and non-athletes in various other fields, speak about being in "The Zone". You have most likely felt this, although you may not have labeled it as such. However, when you have felt this in this past, you have been in that present-moment awareness and you simply lost track of time. The Latin term for this is *"in phasmatis"*, which means, *"in spirit"*.

It is common in most languages to juxtapose three words to describe our goal of a balanced being: *"mind, body and spirit"*. Much has been studied and written throughout history about the connections between mind, body and spirit. Another shortened version that you have surely heard, and maybe even used, is the "mind-body" connection. It is time we re-examine the order in which these three are combined and think of the possible improvements in our search for fulfillment by stating them as "Spirit, Mind and Body".

Although this notion may strike you as mere semantics, it is extremely important, as Tiger pointed out in his interview, that we begin with spirit first. Being in present-moment awareness, in fact, *is* the gateway for us to tap into the *Universal Spirit of Energy* that leads us from *intention* in the spirit, to *attention* of the mind, and subsequently *actions* of the body.

This re-ordering of our approach to fulfillment in everyday life can make a tremendous difference for both our own lives, as well as the lives of others around us. Just the choice of being fully present when you are with someone else opens the energy field between the two, or more, of you that can lead to a spiritual present-moment experience.

As Dr. Deepak Chopra states, in his book *The Seven Spiritual Laws of Success*:

> "....*conscious change is brought about by the two qualities inherent in consciousness: attention and intention. Attention energizes, and intention transforms. Whatever you put your attention on will grow stronger in your life. Whatever you take your attention away from will wither, disintegrate, and disappear. Intention, on the other hand, triggers transformation of energy and information. Intention organizes its own fulfillment. The quality of <u>intention</u> on the object of <u>attention</u> will orchestrate an infinity of space-time events to bring about the outcome intended, provided one follows the other spiritual laws of success. This is because <u>intention</u> in the fertile ground of <u>attention</u> has infinite organizing power. Infinite organizing power means the power to organize an infinity of space-time events, all at the same time. We see the expression of this infinite organizing power in every blade of grass, in every apple blossom; in every cell of our body. We see it in everything that is alive.*"

I would add that *intention* and *attention* also orchestrate infinity of space-time events within the neuroplasticity of our brain, which will be discussed in greater depth in the next chapter.

Yes, we humans have been endowed by our Creator with not only the power of choice, we also have been connected to the *Universal Spirit and Energy* that even allows us to create and be creative. Even our own birth is merely an extension of the actual creative process within the universe. How Blessed is that?

This is powerfully indicated from both Dr. Chopra and Dr. Dyer who come from two distinctly different cultures, religious backgrounds, educations and careers, but who also share common beliefs and experiences of the "spiritual cord" of our parachute. Our parachute *is* the *Universal Spirit and Energy* that gets us to our destiny. Once our choice is made we, then, only have to commit to it *as* our Intention. Again, to paraphrase the spiritual point by Dr. Chopra, "*When we put our* intention...*on the fertile ground of* attention, *it has infinite organizing power and all manner of desires are possible*".

The primary sources for spiritual teachings for most humans are religious doctrines. Fortunately, or, perhaps, unfortunately in some cases, the writing, printing and subsequent interpretation of these divinely inspired doctrines have been crafted by mere mortals.

In this process, we humans sometimes tend to morph what was original intent into our own interpretation. As a result, many who are doing their best to follow their religious doctrines of choice may struggle with the concept of having what Deepak Chopra terms "desires".

When Dr. Chopra, and others, write that "*all manner of desires are possible*", there may be an emotional reaction of disagreement or resistance. But, I invite you to consider that desires are not only a natural element of the human being – and possibly every cell in our being – desires are also fundamental to the achievement of any outcome, even those of the Spirit.

For example, one of the most misunderstood and often confusing areas is on the subject of material wealth. In a CBS Sunday Morning interview, comedian Chris Rock said, "Rich isn't having money. Rich is having options".

The good news about that statement is, for most of us in the developed world, we have plenty of options that start with choices, intention and attention that are available to each of us. But, even if you want to examine the sin vs. virtue of possessing money and its relationship to desires, think of this; using money you have set aside for the specific purpose of helping those less fortunate than yourself can become a "spiritual tool".

I recently watched a pilot series on ABC-TV called "The Secret Millionaire". The producers of this television show sought out extremely successful business people who volunteered to spend a week living in a very impoverished neighborhood, in the same living conditions, and on the same amount of money as most of the people in the neighborhood. For the period of the video taping of the show, their assignment was to go out on the streets and find several organizations or individuals who were volunteering and serving their community on a daily basis. The millionaires were to pass themselves off as volunteers who are doing a documentary on volunteerism.

Once they verified the sincerity of the volunteer work being done and the measurable impact of the work, the "secret millionaire" would then reveal their true identity and donate significant sums of their own money to assist the charitable organizations they have come to know.

In each of the episodes Marilyn and I have watched, both the givers and the receivers are transformed. Considering the challenges of finding worthwhile programming on television, I applauded the ABC Network for being so bold as to actually promote the strong spiritual and "feeling good about giving back" message this show represents. The theme of the show clearly defined the best within us as humans and provided a powerful motivation for being *"in phasmatis"* with our Human Family.

One of my favorite quotes of all time was by a 13-year old Anne Frank. While she was in hiding from Nazi troops in her father's office building during World War II, she wrote, *"How wonderful it is that we need not wait a single moment before starting to improve the world"*.

Under the circumstances she endured on the day she wrote this, it would have been an astonishing comment on the potential of the human spirit by an adult. But, to have been written from the heart of a 13-year old girl is, in my opinion, extraordinary!

This further distinguishes her spiritual and psychological outlook when compared to a generally accepted psychological theory known as the Maslow's Hierarchy of Needs. Dr. Abraham Maslow provided a framework for the human pursuit of fulfillment. Anyone who has studied Maslow's teachings on humanistic psychology will recognize his famous Hierarchy of Needs (Figure 4).

Maslow taught that each of these "needs" had to be satisfied before rising to the next level and, eventually, self-actualization (fulfillment) would be possible. While some argue that Maslow's Hierarchy theory is flawed, most observers have found the theory sound.

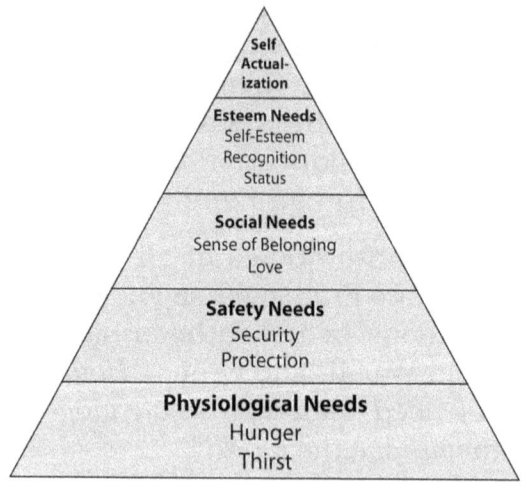

Fig. 4 - Maslow's Hierarchy of Needs

Yet, according to her diary, Anne Frank was generally deprived of the first two foundational needs and was still able to project a spiritual connection to her Human Family, and self-actualized fulfillment. This conclusion was confirmed further when she also wrote, *"I must uphold my ideals, for perhaps the time will come when I shall be able to carry them out"*.

Of course, tragically, we know that she didn't get that chance, but in capturing her spiritual beliefs on paper, she became one of the most influential people who ever lived. Check out her quotes online and you may be surprised at the number of them that are a part of many cultural languages and thoughts today, more than 70 years after she and her sister died of typhus in a concentration camp. We should all aspire to share our spirit with others to that same degree if we value the concept of legacy.

Keep in mind that your legacy doesn't necessarily have to be on the order of the Saints. More often it could be just choosing one or two simple principles that you practice with consistency. These principles become what you are known for and how you touch the lives of others.

A great example of this could be taken from *The Revised Standard Version of the Christian Bible*, Romans 13: verses 8 and 9.

> *8. Owe no one anything, except to love one another, for he who loves another has fulfilled the law.*

9. The commandments, "You shall not commit adultery, You shall not kill, You shall not steal, You shall not covet," and any other commandment, are summed up in this sentence, "You shall love your neighbor as yourself".

Imagine your legacy to be continuously loving to your neighbor as yourself. What impact could it have on the world if you just started with your children and grandchildren, and your friends and neighbors? Why not just start in your immediate surroundings and let that concept spread like a good virus. The best way of creating a legacy is by sharing our time, our thoughts, our deeds and our treasure with others. In doing so, we can create a lifetime of spiritual abundance instead of spiritual limitation.

The challenge is to re-order your *Spirit, Mind, and Body* connections to establish the *intention* of what you want to create as your legacy, and then place your mentally-focused *attention* upon that *intention*. Tuning your Spiritual Cord is both a singularly private and relational experience. This is what we will share as we examine and tune up the Mental Cord of your parachute in the chapter that comes NEXT.

CHAPTER 4
THE MENTAL CORD

"As Iron rusts from disuse, even so does inaction spoil the intellect."

-Leonardo DaVinci

Authors, philosophers, scientists and medical doctors have almost never agreed on, either what the brain truly is, or what its capabilities actually are. There has been agreement, however, that whatever anyone studying the brain thinks it is, they are probably underestimating it. As a result, there have been many attempts, over thousands of years, to find adequate ways to describe various beliefs of the brain's near infinite capabilities. One such analogy that has prevailed over centuries goes like this; if one individual owned all of the sand on all of the beaches on the planet Earth, and used but a cupful, that cupful would equal the amount of the average person's brain capacity that is being used compared to its entire potential.

There are many proven variables in brain fitness and function between different human beings. Also, many have sustained trauma from illness or injury that has damaged the brain. But, what we do know is the "cup of sand" analogy does fit for most humans, even those who have functional challenges or damage to their brains to overcome. This "cup of sand" image presents a stunning visualization for each of us to wrestle with when it comes to analyzing and reflecting on how much of our brainpower or mental function we actually do, or will, utilize.

Although some mention of the brain as an important organ of the human anatomy was first documented approximately 485 B.C., the first study of the brain, with hypotheses as to its function related to the human body, didn't get recorded until approximately 435 B.C. This is when Hippocrates began to speculate the brain might control various specific functions of the body.

But it wasn't until over 2,300 years later, in 1890, that William James (1842 - 1910), the experimental psychologist, author, lecturer and Harvard University professor, first began to teach *"...organic matter, especially nervous tissue, seems endowed with a very extraordinary degree of plasticity"*.

This is a quote from Newsweek's science journalist, Sharon Begley's, book *Train Your Mind, Change Your Brain*. She goes on to state, *"Since (William) James was "only" a psychologist, not a neurologist (there was no such thing as a* neuroscientist over a century ago), his speculation went nowhere. Much more influential was the view expressed succinctly in 1913 by Santiago Ramon y Cajal, the great Spanish neuroanatomist who had won the Nobel Prize in Physiology for Medicine seven years earlier.

Cajal wrote, 'in the adult the nerve paths are something fixed, ended and immutable'. His gloomy assessment that the circuits of the living brain are unchanging, its structures and organization almost as static and stationary as a deathly white cadaver brain floating in formaldehyde, remained the prevailing dogma in neuroscience for almost a century. The textbook wisdom held that the adult brain is hardwired, fixed in form and function, so that by the time we reach adulthood, we are pretty much stuck with what we have."

Conventional wisdom and neuroscience held that the adult mammalian brain could not create new neurons and the functions of the structures that make it up are immutable. There was supposedly sound science behind the "brain charts" that most of us grew up with which colorfully diagrammed the varying structures, or clusters, within the brain that controlled each bodily function.

As an example, it was thought throughout most of the 20th Century, that one particular cortex cluster might only be involved in the movement of the fingers of the right hand, and another cluster controlled the eyesight, while yet another controlled speech, and so on. Thus, mainstream medical science believed they could prove, neurologically, the individual cortex functions of the brain were fixed.

Even as brain functionality, from a physiological point of view, was being progressively revealed over time, there has been an accepted wisdom that all brain function followed a predetermined cycle from birth to death and was "hardwired". It was commonly believed the brain continued to develop throughout childhood and into very early adulthood and then, inevitably the brain would begin a long and slow process of decline and loss of functionality. Also, until the turn of the new millennium, it was commonly believed that if brain cells were injured, damaged or died, they could not be repaired or their function replaced.

Selfishly, my interest in the brain and the scientific realities of neuroplasticity took root after my stroke in 2009. Isn't it interesting how often we take the phenomenal and miraculous for granted until something alarmingly dramatic gets our attention? I have a term for this process which is about coming to recognize the phenomenal and the miraculous through a Significant Emotional Event (SEE). But, even without my SEE "wake-up call" there is this quiet and distant voice that bubbles up within my thoughts from time-to-time and wonders about my brain fitness and function. I occasionally ponder the reliability of my memory and whether I am experiencing that long-held belief of the unavoidable and steady decline of brain functionality.

Maybe you have similar thoughts when some of these events get your attention. When you:

- lose something that was right in front of you only moments before,
- think of a terrific idea only to have it slip away from your recall moments later by the first distraction that comes along, or,
- meet someone you have known for some time and can't remember his or her name.

I have to consciously remember to avoid negative and judgmental thoughts about what these events actually mean. I understand this sort of concern, not just for the most elderly of our population, but that most people in their 40's, 50's, 60's and beyond have fears and concerns about these thoughts (or lost thoughts, in some cases) that crop up occasionally.

The good news for us today is that we now know from proven science that the brain *can* change itself! After so many centuries of what I call "neuro-prejudice," the idea the brain can change itself may sound a bit much for you to embrace, but it is scientifically true, regardless. Thanks to new medical technologies such as functional magnetic resonance imaging (*f*MRI), we can now actually see what is happening in the brain of a living human in real time and track the changes that various stimuli create.

Again, in her book, *Train Your Mind, Change Your Brain*, Sharon Begley writes, "....*in the ripe old age of the 40s, 50's, 60s and, even beyond,* the brain can change its structure and function in a significant way".

How plastic is the Brain?

In the documentary produced for PBS titled "The Brain Fitness Program", the writers and contributors who created the video offer the concept that the brain is both plastic and malleable and is very much subject to influence by many stimuli (for more information or to purchase *The Brain Fitness Program*, go to santafeproductions.com).

The primary contributors include Science Journalist Sharon Begley; Dr. William Jagust, Professor at the University of California-Berkley; Arthur Toga, Professor at UCLA Laboratory of Neuro Imaging; Dr. Michael Merzenich, PhD., of the University of California - San Francisco; Dr. Jason Karlawish, Associate Professor at the University of Pennsylvania; Dr. Norman Doidge, MD, author of *The Brain That Changes Itself* and Dr. Shannon Moffett, Neuro-Researcher and author of *The Three Pound Enigma: The Human Brain and the Quest to Unlock Its Mysteries*.

The consensus offered by these notable authorities concludes that *"...the brain is not hardwired in childhood and we are not doomed by our DNA. On the contrary, our brain is pliable, plastic and subject to change throughout our lifespan, regardless of age or genetics. Brain plasticity has been called one of the most important discoveries of the 20th Century."* These influences can very often be set in motion by the environment we choose; where and how we spend our time, by our sleep patterns, nutrition, our choices about learning, routines, creative pursuits and our attitudes.

Early in life, our brains are in a state of active plasticity and learning. Think about the first time you saw an infant figure out how to accomplish a goal. One that comes to my mind is of a baby who has spent its early months crawling at floor level. One day it is able to crank its head up high enough to spot a shiny object on a coffee table. When it makes the *decision* to go after that shiny object, all of the collected skills its brain has learned are immediately put into use as the baby crawls as fast as it can toward its intended target. When the leg of the table is reached, the baby raises up as it goes hand-over-hand with all if its strength to get to a standing position. Then, without hesitation, the baby grabs the shiny object and its face explodes with pure joy.

Picture what that face exploding with pure joy looks like in your imagination, or memory, because we are going to refer to this mind picture later. This illustrates one of the critical factors to understanding brain function. The thoughts you think have a critical, measurable effect on brain performance. Further, this illustration underscores the power of *intention* and *attention*. (See if you can find the connection to these roles of intention and attention from Chapter 3).

What *The Brain Fitness Program* and an avalanche of new studies are now showing, sheds light on the exciting fact that this sort of learning and the process we all have observed in some area of early life is similar to the story of the baby with the shiny object. It is now known to be possible for all of us, at any age. This alone suggests that we should *rethink what age means to* each of us.

One of the reasons I founded RethinkAge Institute and have, in fact, written this book is to have the opportunity to spread this, and other groundbreaking information. You are challenged to rethink your age, rethink what's possible for you and how you can make the rest of your life the best of your life without the neuro-prejudice of the past holding you back!

It is beyond the practical scope of this book to go into the volumes of research on the question of neuroplasticity and the capacity of the brain to change as a component investigation of mental function and fitness. I hope, however, that I have stimulated your curiosity to at least do some investigation on your own, even if you only procure and study the program and books that are mentioned here. This hope is grounded in the knowledge that when you do, you will discover a whole new world of uplifting possibilities for you to pursue.

Next, I want to offer some tips of what you can do with this sort of research and information.

The 3-Point Brain Fitness Plan

Brain Fitness Plan Point # 1 - Feed the Brain:

There are four primary things you can choose to feed your brain. The first two are oxygen and blood. Deep, cleansing breath is one way to feed your brain with life giving oxygen. The other way is exercise. Yes, exercise!

The first thing your brain needs is a rich combination of oxygen and blood supply. In fact, your blood supply is what delivers oxygen and other nutrients to your brain. And, exercise in almost any form is the absolute, undisputed champion at delivering blood to your brain (more on these benefits in the next chapter).

In the third area, brain nutrition and supplementation, I would direct your attention to the book *Mind Boosting Secrets - Natural Supplements That Enhance Your Mind, Memory and Mood* by Ray Sahelian, MD. He is the expert on feeding your brain, from a nutritional perspective, and I highly recommend you utilize his vast research and experience to formulate your brain nutrition plan. You can find it at raysahelian.com. You can also find his newsletter on that site.

The fourth area of feeding the brain has to do with the *thoughts we choose* and what, in turn, becomes the focus of our *attention*. This fourth area of feeding the brain also has to do with what it takes for us to create learning and positive developmental change in our brain. In fact, it is axiomatic, from a brain physiology perspective, as to how you can rethink your age and choose not to grow *old*. So, please, make sure that you apply your attention to the positive changes that you want to feed yourself as your best chance to manifest your future fulfillment. Your brain will act in the starring role!

Here is how this fourth area of brain function works; whatever you feed your brain in the morning, it will "munch" on all day long. In other words, whatever it is that you focus on, your reality will follow. Where you put your attention is what comes about. Your mind will hold whatever you consistently put into it. By being more critically mindful of what you choose to put into your brain, you can establish the stimulus *diet* that will determine how, in turn, your mind serves your desires for your intended outcome in the future.

Just the process of reading this and other books on this subject and then discussing the concepts presented with others in your "inner circle" is a practice in brain self-development.

I like a quote from motivational speaker and author, Zig Ziglar, who said *"Personal development is like taking a bath. It's not something you want to do every once in a while"*.

Also, think about the four or five people with whom you spend most of your time. When you do invest time with them, its like inviting them into your brain's home. Ask yourself, "Are each of my relationships creating a positive, healthy environment for my brain to 'munch' on"? There can even be a monetary value in creating and maintaining this awareness. Brian Tracy put it into monetary terms when he said, "For every dollar invested in personal development, I've added $30 to my bottom line". More important than money is how your life will turn out as you age.

Remember, we are the directors of the movies of our lives and the brain is the actor waiting for the lines, the cues and the scenes that we invite and trigger. Make sure that what you feed your brain is, by choice, what you truly want as an outcome! For whatever you do feed your brain, will become your reality.

Remember also that aging, if you are lucky, is inevitable, but getting *old* is your choice!

Brain Fitness Plan Point # 2 - Exercise the Brain:

One of my favorite sayings is "*a rut is just a grave with both ends kicked out*". Until I began paying more attention to brain fitness and functionality, I didn't really realize the real truth in this statement. One of the most interesting, and potentially damaging, characteristics of humans is that we all tend to gravitate toward the known, or routine. We find comfort there in doing what is known or easiest. But, there are huge prices to pay for this comfort of routine.

The first price is the actual loss of function within our neurons and their neurotransmitters. By continuously, and for some, tenaciously, clinging to what the brain already knows, the "plasticity switches" for those skills or thought patterns are turned off, and nothing changes in the brain. Also, we direct our brains to switch from a learning mode to a utility mode which triggers a completely different functionality and somewhat reduces the amount of attention demanded of the brain.

Continued over a long period of time, the developed habit of clinging to the known, removes the sense of wonder, energy and spark from our daily lives as the same routines are played over and over. This begins a process of limiting the person that you become and causes your world to *shrink*, leaving only a mere shell of your real potential.

The second price to be paid for your "rut" is the absence of growth! It is, therefore, critical that you keep stimulating and feeding your brain with creative pursuits, continuous learning, stimulating exercise and discovery of your unknown. The beneficial bonuses will be the continuous manifestation of your native and innate longing for fulfillment.

Brain Fitness Plan Point # 3 - Challenge the Brain:

We can now see that it is also crucial to challenge the brain by learning new skills and information. Once learned, we must also work on reinforcing the skills or information in order for the learning of it to have any lasting effect. If you have ever decided to learn a new language, you know what this means. Again, the *use it or lose it* principal kicks in and it is no different for any new skill or information that you acquire. Simple, but often repeated stimuli, such as environment and behavior, actually tunes the region of the brain required for that repetitive function. The lesson here is to choose carefully what stimuli you expose to your brain.

So, what will your challenge be? How will you test all of this information you have just acquired by selecting the next thing you are committed to learn? Learning is not a spectator sport. But, as you do get on the field of play in brain and mental fitness and function, I would offer this word of caution; practice *doesn't* make perfect. Practice makes whatever you practice permanent!

As the principal player in your own game of life, you must be the chief participant and then practice what you want to make permanent. But remember, once it becomes permanent in your routine, it's time to stretch out and develop something new. This brings us back to my favorite "four-letter-word," NEXT!

One of the most interesting new tools for figuring out what your challenge will be, and how you might test all of the information presented in this chapter, would be for you to explore the use of mind mapping. Although Tony Buzan created the *iMindMapping* software in December,

2006, he points to the practice as having been used by the ancient geniuses in nearly all fields of study throughout history.

Mr. Buzan states that mind mapping is a thinking tool that reflects externally what goes on inside your head. He likes to say that *"it is like a Swiss Army knife for the brain"*. The brain takes a thought, idea or concept, and explodes it outwardly in radial branches.

As opposed to the habits of many who take notes or make lists in a linear fashion, mind mapping branches are a reflection of the way that the brain actually *thinks*. The brain takes a topic of thought and thinks of it in terms of imagination and association. The reason why traditional note taking and lists are less effective than mind mapping is that we don't have the associations. Without association there is less, or sometimes no, connection. If you don't have operative connections, there is less memory building and less constructive thinking.

In a mind map the branches are always curved. Mr. Buzan teaches that if all of the branches were straight they would be more rigid and, therefore, result in the brain *getting bored and unhappy*. But, with mind mapping, the brain becomes more absorbed and intrigued. If you would like to learn more about mind mapping, I recommend that you look into thinkbuzan.com for more information.

Fresh Perspectives

If I asked you if you need your brain you would say 'of course' and may even think the question to be frivolous. But, what about this question, "Does your brain need *you?*" Surely the answer is still "yes" but who is *you*, separate from your brain?

Dr. Deepak Chopra has written that many people feel we are human beings who have occasional spiritual experiences. But, he maintains we are spiritual beings who have occasional human experiences. I agree.

My layman's research into the brain has helped me create awareness and a conclusion I have not explored before. There is a co-dependency between ourselves and our brains that goes beyond the obvious, or what we have been taught in school. As I mentioned before, your brain is the actor and you are the director.

Remembering previous references to *spirit-mind-body*, we, the spiritual being, choose the thoughts, intentions, desires and that on which we will put our attention. Then, the neurotransmitters signal clusters of neurons to fulfill our wishes. Whether that means translate speech, solve a problem at work or at home, moving part or all of our body or creating a symphony, our brain usually delivers – and often with amazing speed and accuracy. So what does our brain need from us in return? It needs stimulation, exercise and nutrients to continue to operate at a peak level with healthy mental function and fitness.

Once you have made the decision – no, the commitment – that you are going to give your brain the new attention it deserves, and you are now ready to act on that commitment, the next thing is to take a look at the role your physical fitness and vital health plays in this amazing opportunity we have called "being human".

CHAPTER 5
THE PHYSICAL CORD

"Discipline is the bridge between goals and accomplishment."

- Jim Rohn

Since the beginning of recorded history, many of the ancient religious and philosophical teachings tell us our bodies are our home, or temple, within which our spirit resides. Therefore, we must keep this a sacred place from which to operate in the physical world. You have been exposed to many kinds of messages about the importance of good health and fitness all of your life. You know that it makes common sense to keep your physical fitness and health in tip-top operating condition.

I am not sure who said "You should take extraordinary care of your body because, well, where else are you going to live?", but it is a concept that is hard to deny. You absolutely know that it is better to feel good, energetic and alive than it is to feel bad, sick, tired and lethargic. All of this is surely abundantly clear and, therefore, we should not need a repeat lesson on the virtues of physical fitness and health at any age, right? Well, not so fast!

I am grateful to live within a few miles of a YMCA facility which is well equipped with an aerobic room that contains 12 programmable treadmills, eight elliptical machines, two stair stepper machines, a rowing machine and six stationary bicycles. We have a separate circuit training room with 17 stations. We have a serious weight room and both indoor basketball and racquetball courts. We also have an outdoor swimming pool and an indoor running track. Obviously, this is a wonderful facility. But why am I telling you all of these working statistics? Well, in my small town there are approximately 35,000 residents who are within easy driving distance of this facility. Even with the low number of stations, compared to the number of potential resident users, what is amazing to me, and some of my exercise friends, *we never have to wait on a machine or weights*! Now I do know that not everybody even wants to exercise, much less first thing each morning, which is my preference. Also, there are two other exercise facilities in town. But just think about it. Over 35,000 people and, no waiting! What's wrong with this picture?

What is even more troubling to me about this observation has to do with what I call the "resolutioners". The first week of every January the gym does get more crowded. It starts to look like we may actually have to wait for a minute or two on some stations. But, the regulars know that all we have to do is be patient and then, sure enough, by the third week of January it all goes back to normal. That's about when most resolutioners lose their motivation about their New Year's convictions. The first time they have some sort of conflict of schedule, or they get sore, or sleeping-in sounds like a better option, or they are so tired at the end of their long working days... well, you know the rest.

In recent years, even the resolutioners have stopped showing up. This year there was a very minimal impact of only a few more than the regulars in the facility in January, and those few only stayed for a week or two. I have to wonder if this is a reflection of a whole new level of apathy, or, "why bother?" attitude that comes from a fundamental shift in the human psyche.

And, it's not just in America. In my work with Rotarians around the world, they report the same phenomenon in their countries, too! In most developed countries of the world, there seems to be a gradual shift to thinking and playing smaller than before; a sense of lower expectations.

Maybe you have noticed it also. Is it because our various societies feel they have been beaten up by the complexities of challenging economies, complex technological and social times and more and more demands that people are feeling? Maybe it's just that there is a prevailing disenchantment with believing in something that people have already decided doesn't work – or at least is not possible for them – like New Year's Resolutions, permanent weight loss or extraordinary health and fitness!

Actually, it doesn't matter what it may be for society in general. Let's change society, one person at a time, beginning with a focus on what *you*, as a free-willed, choice-making and independent thinker can do for *you*. The most challenging of times is *exactly* when we need to seek to raise ourselves to a higher standard of excellence and to seek the keys to peak performance. I have experienced what it is like to ignore my own physical health and fitness, while, at the same time, believing that I was doing just fine. This can happen to anyone and it can happen, slowly, subtly and without overt warning signs at any stage of life.

At the age of 35, I ended a marriage of 13 years, was single and a workaholic. For the previous five-and-a-half years I had been buried in my office or on airplanes every week with a Detroit, Michigan-based company. I had responsibility for the company's operations in the United States and Canada. After months of my non-stop schedule, Jack, the owner of the company, suggested I take a break. He owned a condominium in Acapulco and said he wanted to take me there to get away and rest up for a week.

The day we arrived, he had his housekeeper take a photo of Jack and me. We were out on his balcony in our bathing suits, posing with the typical tropical drinks in our hands. The main Acapulco beachfront skyline was in the distant background. We went on to have a great week and I did come back feeling much more rested and energized.

About two weeks later, Jack walked into my office and gave me a set of photo prints from our trip that he had developed. I smiled and thanked him for his thoughtfulness and also for the trip opportunity. I pulled the prints from the envelope and there they were! Right there on top of the stack were two different shots of Jack and me in those bathing suits. I almost didn't recognize myself!

Ever since high school I have been somewhat tall, at about 6'2", and slimly built. It is the way I always "saw" myself. But, this guy staring back at me with this drink in his hand was huge with the most prominent feature being my belly!

How did this happen to me? I thought back to the last couple of times that I had bought clothes and then remembered I had noticed some *minor* changes in size and the snugness of my pants each time. But, in reflection, I always thought it was the manufacturer, or something else but, surely, it was not me!

My photo-aided shock led to a decision. The decision led to commitment. I joined a gym and hired a coach. On my first day in the gym, he weighed and measured me. I weighed 245 pounds and had a 41-inch waist. I couldn't do more that four sit-ups, about eight push-ups, and couldn't lift much of any weight at all.

So, I went to work with a passion (highly recommended). I dramatically changed my diet and travel schedule. Within six months, I was on a heavy protein diet and nearly lifting my own body weight in many of the exercises. I had dropped my weight to 195 pounds and had a 36-inch waist.

At the age I was then, the good news (and bad news,) about doing this was my body was reacting to the extreme workout program in a very dramatic way. In fact, I realized that I had gone too far one day in about my eighth month of heavy lifting when I went into the locker room after a particularly grueling upper body workout to discover that the muscles in my arms, chest, shoulders and lats were so engorged with blood and swollen tissue that I couldn't take off my tank top shirt by myself. I had become so *pumped up* that I literally could not reach around my upper body to grab my shirt or reach over my shoulders to grab the back of it. This was embarrassing! I had to ask another guy in the locker room to help me take my shirt off. "OK. Enough!", I said. Either extreme is not good.

This story was shared just to let you know that I have actually experienced both extremes of physical fitness and strength. But, I have also experienced both extremes in physical health. Other than having the flu so bad that I thought I would have to die to improve, my lowest point was when

I had my small stroke in October of 2009. As a result, I was told that I would probably be on my three new medications for the rest of my life.

But, one of my highest points was December 2010, when I was able to drop all three medications. I have the blood pressure of a teenager and my muscles are responding well to my current training. Also, my energy levels are rising on a progressive basis each month. All of this is a result of my training, nutritional assimilation and the other health habits that I count now on, and to which I am committed. The really good news is I am not any more special or gifted than most of you reading this.

So, what does distinguish the difference in fitness results between humans? I am sure that some of you reading this are saying, "Oh sure, you may be able to do this but I have tried everything and nothing seems to work"! Or, "I am genetically predisposed to this or that issue because that is what happens in my family". Throughout most of my adulthood I have invested a lot of money and time trying to understand this seeming disparity, myself.

My conclusion:

Making a significant positive change in your physical fitness starts within your spirit and mind!

Another of the many reasons that we are as very blessed as humans is, unlike machines, we are not limited by finite capacities. Roger Bannister, born March 23, 1929, in Harrow, Middlesex, England, grew up, as he says, "not knowing luxury".

He didn't start foot racing until age 17. This was considered a relatively late age to begin in this highly competitive sport. At that time, no human, in recorded history, had ever run a mile in less than four minutes.

As Bannister states in his memoirs, *The Four-Minute Mile*, published in 1955, the sportswriters during that period were mostly responsible for helping create the myth that this feat was *humanly impossible*, since many gifted athletes had tried and, although some came close, had never been able to achieve the supposedly impossible goal.

On the 6th of May 1954, Roger represented Oxford University in a track meet in front of 3,000 people. The wind was blowing at average of 25 miles per hour and Roger decided not to run so that he could save himself for another upcoming race. But, just before the one-mile race was to start, the wind calmed and he changed his mind. It was a very close race with only a couple of seconds separating the top three runners, but Roger finished first (Figure 5), with an all-time record of 3 minutes, 59.4 seconds, becoming the first person in history to break the "impossible" four-minute mile.

Fig. 5 - Roger Bannister breaking the record for a one mile race in less than four minutes.

One inescapable fact of interest is, in the years that have followed his "impossible" accomplishment, many others have also been able to run a sub-four-minute mile race. What is it about human beings that could make this happen?

How is it we can take the *impossible* and make it achievable?

Roger Bannister later stated, "Breaking the four-minute mile was more of a psychological than a physical matter. The man, who drives himself further, once the going gets painful, is the man who will win". He completed medical school at Oxford University and was later knighted by Queen Elizabeth for his record breaking run.

At 82, Sir Roger is still in medical practice as a neurologist in England. Referring to medicine and neurologic health, he recently said, "... (after racing) I undertook a deliberate challenge to learn everything about medicine which I could never achieve. I think it is very good to be put in your place in that way."

It seems that the same motivation that helped him become that record-breaking young athlete is still working for him today as he continuously challenges and stimulates his *Spirit, Mind and Body* to achieve aliveness in his intentions.

I may never get the chance to meet Sir Roger Bannister. However, I am privileged to personally know someone who shares his code of peak performance. My friend is Patrick "Pat" Johns.

Pat is an international motivational speaker; world class athlete who has run the Himalayan 100-mile race four times, and the only journalist to do so. Pat explained, in the early 1900's, the Aga Kahn, ruled much of India. Khan had heard of a place where it was possible to see *four giants* and he wanted a way to get there; a way to see for himself. So, at some point in his reign he said "build me a trail".

The giants are four of the tallest peaks in the world known as Mt. Everest, Lotse, Makalu and Kantchanjunga. Much of The Himalayan 100-mile race is run in extremely high altitudes on the Kahn's old rock-strewn trail, which serves as the border between India and Nepal.

For the last 15 years, the race and this trail have attracted some of the world's most elite endurance runners. As an athlete, adventure journalist and motivational speaker, Pat first went there in 2000 to understand the core values of this highly motivated group of people who would run this course. What he discovered gives us the clues to our own higher performance potential. His discovery, which he now speaks about as one of his core keynote presentations, is what he calls the Five C's: Leaving your Comfort zone, Commitment, Connection, Common Sense and Compassion.

To learn more about Pat and the Himalayan 100-mile race, visit his website at patjohns.com. On that website, you will find a KERA/NPR interview to which you can listen as Pat describes each phase of this truly amazing race.

Pat shared his experience with me saying, "The key to a human accomplishing positive change in any undertaking requires starting with a spiritual *mindfulness* that deals with limiting beliefs and fears by putting them into perspective". Pat said an example of the self-talk required to create a more positive *mindfulness* is, "Is this going to kill me? Oh, probably not, it just may be uncomfortable in the beginning. Then, we must have strong enough belief in the outcome so that when the going *does* get uncomfortable, we don't quit!"

Do you hear any parallels between Pat's learned perspective and Sir Roger Bannister's? Pat indicated that most people, in all walks of life or endeavor quit too early and often, just before they would have broken through to success. Pat believes this goes against the Laws of Nature. Think of plants growing, birds flying, ocean tides and all forms of new life in nature. All other forms of nature around us do not quit. It is mostly we humans who *think* our way out of doing something.

Next he said using his Five C's makes all the difference. He went on to share a brief look at what he means:

C #1: **Comfort Zone** - We must be willing to leave our comfort zone and begin our growth process by recognizing the fear and determining its validity, or lack thereof.

C #2: **Commitment** - Pat encourages us to speak of and share our intentions *loud and clear.* Peer pressure can be a positive force when your peers are helping you stay focused on your intentions. By putting your intentions into a verbal commitment you can create partner energy that sets many other possibilities in motion, and may have never been available to you if you had kept your intentions only within yourself.

C #3: **Connection** - We have touched on this in the Spiritual Cord chapter by focusing on being *present* with what is going on in *this moment*. Unfortunately, negative examples of what happens without a connected presence are all around us every day; driving accidents, hospital errors or physicians prescribing medications in a potentially dangerous way.

Not long ago, I saw a mother followed by her two pre-school aged children, walking across a busy and high-traffic driveway at a store. As she was totally absorbed with texting and walking on into the store, her two small children lagged behind in car traffic by themselves.

Tragically, every year babies and small children suffocate to death from heat and lack of fresh air after having been thoughtlessly left locked in their parents' vehicles. So, being in connection with what we are doing, being present in that moment, is not only a great way to begin and succeed at any task, it can often be a matter of life or death!

A positive aspect of connection goes back to present-moment awareness for the activity at hand. It can be as simple as sharing a moment with a loved one or being in "The Zone".

C #4: **Common Sense** - This is often nothing more than trusting your own intuition about what works and what doesn't. You have the power of choice to believe in yourself and that old saying that, "God doesn't make junk"! If you were not endowed with a substantial amount of common sense, you probably wouldn't be alive to read this. There is a tendency, however, among many people to let their fears, doubts and worries overshadow their own common sense. Once you have committed to a course of thinking or action, just trust that common sense will provide the course corrections along the way – when you listen to it – and, you will arrive at your destination. This is especially true when all of the cords on your parachute are attended to and in balance.

C #5: **Compassion** - We are in a constant battle between the left side of the brain, the side that wants to analyze and control and the right side of the brain which seeks creative unity and connection to the full range of possibilities. You can consciously choose to give preference to the right side of your brain and, in doing so, unleash extraordinary power and energy that will serve you well.

So many people around the world today have only a win/lose mentality. For them, winning is the only thing and just the love of competition – winning or not – has no place in their psyche. But, think about it! Being compassionate for others does not mean being weak. In fact, being compassionate is quite the opposite. It takes strength of spirit and mind to show compassion to others while understanding the positive energy flow which is created between beings because of that act.

These are the principals that Pat Johns teaches and by which he lives that have led him to his peak performance. I appreciate his willingness to share it with me, and now with you.

And, now I will share my own story with you. Remember me telling you about my fitness coach, Jeff? When I first began working with Jeff, he had me send him a description of the training that I was doing at that time, including a list of exercises, weights and repetitions.

After reviewing my exercise plan, mostly involving weights, Jeff asked me a question for which I was unprepared. He asked, "Did you know that you are only doing 25 percent of peak physical fitness"?

My answer was that I didn't know what he is talking about. In that moment, I was thinking, "I'm working hard three days a week lifting weights and I'm only achieving 25 percent of peak physical fitness"? So, I asked him to explain.

Jeff informed me that physical fitness – complete physical fitness – requires us to be constantly improving four areas of training. The first, but only 25 percent, is *strength* to which I was attending. However, he went on to say the other three areas are *endurance*, *flexibility* and something he called *responsive agility*.

I understood what he meant by the first three areas but I did not understand what he meant by the fourth, *responsive agility*.

He explained that by having me imagine I was on the floor doing a project, or playing with a child, and the phone rang. Responsive agility is being able to rise up and answer the phone in one fluid motion, without the accompanying aches, pains or hesitations. I got it! As a result of this conversation, Jeff helped me begin a completely redesigned training program that was aimed at accomplishing all four of the areas of which he spoke.

My new and continuous training program involves a six-day-per-week regimen of equally balanced aerobic (builds health) and anaerobic (builds muscle) training. Jeff also has me doing calisthenics, yoga and stretching first thing each morning before going to the gym. I call this program "Waking up Wonderfully!" This type of mindset is an important part of the training, as well. I also change the training regularly and encourage you to do the same.

One of the primary reasons that people give up going to a training facility is boredom. I heard once that "you can only be bored in the absence of a new idea". So *surprising* your *spirit, mind and body,* with new ideas that target the same areas and results, will keep you going for a long, long time.

For me, this training program works and is a much more extraordinary way to begin each day than sleepily munching and drinking my way through a donut and coffee. I am also going to bed earlier, sleeping great and waking up with energy to spare! This type of natural health energy lasts me much longer throughout the day than the energy induced by stimulants like caffeine and sugar.

Understanding that each of us are different in gender, age, size, physical conditioning and general health, prevents me from offering you specific advice regarding a training program that might be ideal for you compared to what is working for me. But, if the description of what is working for me sounds good to you, the fundamentals are available to members of the RethinkAge Institute, which can be found at RethinkAge.com.

I do feel both comfortable and qualified to share with you some fundamental principles I found to be true in my years of study and research since my weight related and photo-triggered wake-up call over 33 years ago.

Of all the advice, learning, research and practical experience that I can offer, this I know for certain, our *spiritual intention* combined with an *extraordinary commitment* with which you view your physical body and health is the best beginning point. Doesn't it just make sense to pursue an intention of extraordinary physical fitness, health and a vital feeling of aliveness?

When you begin to use your new *intention* to become the *victor* with extraordinary fitness and not the *victim* of poor fitness, you wake up feeling energetic every day. Once you begin to place your *attention* on the *intention* of extraordinary physical fitness, the neurotransmitters in your brain will recruit the necessary neurons to move you in the direction of finding the best solutions for you and you will get the motivation to create the transformation that you intend.

Remember that our creative brain thinks in imagery and association. As just one fitness challenge-related example, let's take a look at the intention to lose weight. Our brains *cannot create the imagery* of *losing weight*. However, our brains can picture us being a different size or shape.

I have a drawing from a golf training text I have chosen to use to illustrate my image goal of the ideal example for my body frame and type. This illustration is taped to my bathroom mirror and I use it to create the imagery of what peak physical fitness looks like for me.

So I ask you, "What are the dominating habits of thought that are on your mind when you look in the mirror?" Whatever that habitual thought is for you will determine the consistent message with which you are training your brain and, without prejudice, your brain will respond by getting you as close to what you are imagining and associating with as it can. I call this the *adaptive response* and it all operates on what you choose to think.

Choose, and then commit to, your own ideally desired image to use as an *adaptive response*.

Then it's time to write it all down in a daily training plan (notice I have not mentioned *working out* or *daily exercise*). By writing it down, you will have a *specific training plan to follow each day* that will form your thought habits and train your brain and body to expect the demands you know will make a difference for you over time.

Is FAT My Friend or My Enemy?

In the world of private pilots there is a well known saying that goes like this, "There are old pilots and there are bold pilots, but, there are no old bold pilots". The older a pilot gets and the more experience they accumulate, the more they respect the training, procedures, cautions and awareness it takes to get to be an even older pilot.

There is a parallel among all humans when it comes to *fat* and there is no pun intended when I say that this is, indeed, a huge issue. In fact, you don't have to be exposed to any news media for long without seeing or hearing an alarming story of the rapidly growing population of people who are obese in developed nations. Of course, obese is the politically correct word for what you and I know as *fat*. The parallel saying could be, "There are old people and there are fat people, but there are not many old fat people".

A friend of mine shared this idea with me and the more I thought about it, the more sense it made. Do you know any very elderly people? Do you know any very elderly people who are also very *fat*? Probably not! And, that is about as motivational a revelation as anyone should need for active fitness.

There is an incredible array of physical health and fitness books, CDs and DVDs for every level of training that you would like to create. I strongly urge you to research the possibilities online and find the right one for you. A book that I feel comfortable in recommending for anyone at any level of training experience is *Live Young Forever - 12 Steps to Optimum Health, Fitness & Longevity* by Jack LaLanne. Jack wrote this book at age 95 in 2009.

Francois Henri "Jack" LaLanne (1914 – 2011) was an American fitness, exercise and nutritional expert and motivational speaker who is sometimes called "the godfather of fitness" and the first American "fitness superhero". He opened one of the nation's first fitness gyms in 1936 at the age of 21.

For the next 75 years, Jack worked tirelessly to impress the value of fitness upon the people of the world. When you get his book, you will be surprised at all of the near *super-human* feats he performed to get people to pay attention to what fitness can do at any age. I am quite certain, if pneumonia had not claimed his life, he would still be training today.

The book covers more than training. It also is an inspirational source of information on the value of motivation, planning, curing damaging habits, personal care, nutrition, posture, hydration, assimilation of nutrients, elimination of waste, stretching, retirement and attitudes about life in general.

One of his famous quotes was, "Good habits are the key to success". Jack's good habits helped him self-actualize his dream that "while he walked this earth, he was marvelously alive"! You have the power of choice and, hopefully, now the motivation to live your life the same way – *marvelously alive*!

> **Caution:** *While I share the stories of Sir Roger Bannister, Pat Johns, and Jack LaLanne to illustrate the extreme performance of which the body is capable, I certainly do not wish for you to judge yourself in comparison to these, or any other champions of physical fitness. Also it is very important that you seek the counsel, and approval, of your physician prior to making any changes in your nutrition, exercise or training regimen. Although you may know your body better than anyone else, the small amount of time and money that it takes to consult a medical or chiropractic professional is a great investment toward your peace of mind and well-being.*

CHAPTER 6
THE VITAL HEALTH CORD

"Anything in life is possible, and YOU make it happen."
- *Jack LaLanne*

All my life I have heard, "Without good health, nothing else matters". That's hard to argue with, isn't it? And, yet, I feel confident that you and I have both had to live with the consequences of poor health choices. Wouldn't it be nice if we could somehow be immune from the consequences of our poor health choices? In this chapter, I want to share a few simple common sense concepts that I have found to be easy to follow and have made into powerfully positive and vital habits. These habits have been very meaningful in pursuit of physical fitness and vital health in my life.

RethinkAge Institute's
FIVE MAGIC PILLARS OF VITAL HEALTH

As people go through their daily routines, one of the things they think about early and often is what there is to eat. Take a moment and reflect on the kinds of foods you think about and consume most often.

The next most common thing that people start thinking about consuming throughout their day is something to drink. Please pause for a moment, when you start to think of something you normally drink. What comes to mind? Is it coffee, tea, soft drinks, fruit juices, alcoholic beverages or maybe even water?

Once you load up each day on food and drink, the next thing that becomes a necessary part of the day is we cleanse our bodily systems through the elimination of any waste that accumulates. Does this happen for you in your daily routine or is this process something that you would like to be working in a more efficient and balanced manner?

One of the things that people seldom think about throughout their day is air. What sort of deep cleansing breathing habits have you developed?

Last is an aerobic (with oxygen) and anaerobic (without oxygen, normally resistance training) program that keeps your body challenged and your spirit, mind and body thriving with enthusiastic energy.

Let's think of the priority you currently give to these critical bodily processes in another way. How long you can function and stay healthy without providing for your body's needs may give us a clue as to what and how much attention we should give to each of those needs.

I call this process of creating your awareness of the natural design priority of your body the "Survivability Factor". This means that when you prioritize and attend to what your body needs most for survival, in accordance with which functions need your attention and care in the shortest amount of time, you have shifted your focus to the Survivability Factor for that particular bodily need. The primary examples of this order of attention are as follows:

1) How long can you go without air? Is it 30 seconds, 60 seconds, 90 or 120 seconds before you cannot hold your breath any longer? Do you know how much damage is caused to your system is caused as a result?

2) How long can your body go without water before damage is done to your tissue and organs? Possibly just 48 hours?

3) How long can your body go without food?   Is it days?

4) How long do you think your body could function without the elimination of

accumulated waste before discomfort and disease set in?

5) How long can your body go without aerobic or anaerobic training? You may have already proven to yourself you could go for a lifetime without physical training of any kind. The real significant questions become, how long would you like for your lifetime to last? And, what would the quality of your life be, either with, or without aerobic and anaerobic physical training? A well balanced aerobic and anaerobic training plan that you consistently complete each week can also be the difference between just physically surviving and *thriving*.

The point I am making is that our bodies are already organized to signal us with what we need most by how long we can go without attending to the signals of our body's requirements. The real challenge is that we just don't pay any attention to this design order and what I call the Pillars of Vital Health.

Just by paying attention to our own bodily needs we should get the message loud and clear that there is an *order* in which the *Five Magic Pillars of Vital Health* require our attention, based upon which of them we need the soonest. Using those criteria, the order of priority for what we should give our attention to is: first – air (breathing), second – water (hydration) third

– food (nutrition), fourth – eliminating waste and toxins from our bodies and fifth – aerobic and anaerobic physical training and conditioning. So let's take a practical look at each one.

Vital Health Pillar Number 1 - AIR: You may ask, "What's the big deal? We breathe unconsciously and automatically, right? Why all the fuss? I've been doing it since birth?" Here's the big deal: *Oxygen* is the source of all energy in the body. Cells use Oxygen to convert glucose into adenosine triphosphate (ATP). Your cells make up *all* of your body and they *all* need oxygen.

Oxygen comes from the air you breathe. The higher the quality of deep, cleansing breaths, the greater the chances of oxygen doing the necessary fueling of the cells in your body, including the brain and its nervous system, the circulatory system, the organs, muscle and skin tissues. The fact that we breathe automatically actually lowers our awareness of the need for these deep cleansing breaths. And, therein, lies the danger over our lifetimes.

Most of us are never aware of our breathing. Since we are so busy living our lives in so many other areas of interest (like food), breathing becomes victim to the least effort we can consciously put into it. As a result, we have the tendency to breathe with only the upper portion of our lungs, normally less than half, and we even do that with short soft and shallow breaths. But, stop and think of the clue about how long you can go without breathing. Doesn't that tell you something about what priority breathing in healthy doses of oxygen should have in your health consciousness?

For most people, the only time we take deep breaths is when we are in physical exertion or yawning, both of which are involuntary demands that our bodies initiate to increase oxygen flow. The habit of shallow and limited breathing is taking a huge toll on the function of our bodies. But, it is a silent toll and we don't feel it; there's not any pain involved so it must not be important (like hunger pains). You may be surprised at the lists of bodily functions you can improve by providing greater volumes of oxygen to your cellular system.

Here is a sample of those benefits:

1. High levels of energy, alertness and vitality

2. Strong and positive functioning heart and respiratory system

3. An overall sense of well-being

4. Reduction of numbness and cramps in arms, legs, hands, neck, shoulders and back

5. Reduction in digestive issues

6. Improved cognitive skills and brain function

7. Improved sleep

8. Improved cellular health and function

Consider this: those of us who regularly practice the deepest breathing may be the ones that live the longest. So, breathe!

A good pattern of breathing which maximizes oxygen into your system is the "4 - 8 - 16 X 4" pattern. Take in as much deep cleansing breath through your nose as you can as you count out 4 seconds. Then hold your breath for a count of 8 seconds. Finish with slowly exhaling through your mouth for a count of 16 seconds. Then repeat three more times for a total of 4 sets. Repeat this hourly throughout your day. It is simple, effective and energy boosting. If this pattern causes you to become light headed at first, just use the same ratios and work your way up to these counts of endurance from a smaller beginning number (e.g. - 2 - 4 - 8 X 2).

Now where does breathing in oxygen fit into your health plan?

Vital Health Pillar Number 2 - Cleansing and Health Giving Hydration: This subject, like oxygen, deserves its own book. It is that important! However, I will just share with you some brief points that will hopefully inspire you to dive into your own research and create a plan to improve the way you hydrate. Water, not any other form of liquid, is essential to the health and well-being of almost all living organisms.

A full 75 percent of our body's weight, including our brain, is due to water. In addition to providing the basis for life in virtually every cell of our body, most major bodily processes or functions cannot occur without it. This includes the movement of muscle, our circulatory system, digestion and the elimination of waste and toxins. In addition to serving as a transporter for nutrients throughout our bodies, water also is a basic building and repair material for the body as well as helping control body temperature.

One thing that you may not realize is that we are losing water constantly when we go through our normal daily routines of breathing, perspiring to cool the body, urination, digestion and bowel movements.

In case these benefits are not motivating enough to cause you to rethink the amount of water you might consume, water is also known to be an effective tool to use for weight loss. In addition to creating a sensation of *being full*, an increase in water consumption can also suppress your appetite and even accelerate metabolizing of stored body fat and reduce fat deposits.

With all of these functions of the human body being so critically and positively reliant upon water, wouldn't it make sense that each of us gave more than a passing thought to hydrating only when our mouth gets dry? Well, like most everything else we've been discussing, proper hydration requires thoughtful planning – actually training! So let's begin by helping you figure out how much hydration is right for you.

The best rule of thumb that I have found in my research and one that works very well for me, is that we should ideally consume one half of our total body weight in pounds converted to ounces of water each day.

Here is what that formula looks like with the following examples:

- Body weight 200 pounds/divided by half = 100 ounces,
- 100 ounces divided by 12-ounce glasses = 8.33 glasses/day,

or

- Body weight 120 pounds divided by half = 60 ounces, 60 ounces divided by 12-ounce glasses = 5 glasses/day

I keep a one liter glass bottle of water on my desk. From the time I get up, until I go to bed each night, I consume approximately three liters per day. One liter is equal to 34 US fluid ounces. So the 100, or so, ounces of hydration per day more than covers me for my weight of 185. Now it's your turn to use this formula:

- Body weight ____ divided by 2 = ____ ounces,
- Ounces divided by 12 ounce glasses = ____ glasses/day (or divided by 34 ounces = ____ liters per day)

(CAUTION: - If you have not been consuming water in the volumes reflected in this formula, work up to the full formula application slowly over a period of one or two weeks,

and as always, consult your physician prior to any major jump into a different routine).

When you start each day with a full glass of water, and then train yourself to create awareness about all of the health giving and necessary functions that your water intake is providing for you, it is not such a daunting task. When it becomes a habit, everything will work better for you. Some people might object to the inevitable result that they are going to the bathroom more often as a result of an increase in water consumption.

What we all need to understand is there are even two huge *bonus benefits* to this seemingly inconvenient outcome. First, is the benefit of you becoming more effective in regularly getting rid of the toxins that normally accumulates in your body. Second, the act of getting up and moving about, even for this reason, has a positive effect on your body as opposed to sitting or maintaining a certain position for extended periods of time. Isn't it good to know that going to the bathroom is actually so beneficial?

Vital Health Pillar Number 3 - Food and Nutrition: What primate is the strongest on the planet, pound for pound? If you guessed a silverback mountain gorilla, you are correct. In the thick forests of central and West Africa, troops of gorillas find plentiful food for their vegetarian diet. They eat roots, shoots, fruit, wild celery, tree bark and pulp. I am not a vegetarian, nor do I recommend or discourage anyone from becoming one. Neither am I suggesting that we should eat what the silverback gorillas eat.

Obviously, the food they eat provides great nutrition for them. But, the primary food lessons we can learn from these animals is their diet also provides four other essentials for their strength and health that may not be so obvious:

1. Nearly everything they eat has high *water content*.
2. Everything they eat is fresh, raw and *not cooked*.
3. Everything they eat tends to be more *alkaline* than acidic.
4. Everything they eat is *organic* (without pesticides).

There is *serious, life-giving* information here. All of us have been told we should eat more fresh vegetables, fruits and foods that don't contain chemicals or pesticides. The near revolutionary growth in the awareness of organically grown foods has become a phenomenon in most developed nations.

No matter where you may fall in the debate over vegetarian or the organic spectrum of what to purchase and eat, the lessons from the silverback gorilla that deserve your thoughtful attention are the high *water* content of their diet, the fresh *uncooked* nature of their diet and the *high alkalinity/low acidity* of their diet.

When you really think about it, the *vast* majority of the processed and manufactured food we consume isn't designed for this same kind of healthy outcome. It is designed for speed, convenience, lengthening shelf life or price. If you use your common sense about the textural, ingredient and chemical make up of what you are ingesting, you will know that most of our population has drifted far, far away from what our bodies can process effectively.

So, here are a couple of worthy questions you can use as vital health decision filters for what you are about the insert into your mouth for your body's system to deal with:

1. Is what I am about to pass over my lips going to *clog* or *cleanse* my body?

2. Is my long term health, energy and vitality more important to me than the temporary taste, comfort or convenience that comes with what I am thinking of consuming?

You intuitively know the right answers. You also know it is within your power to discipline yourself to make the decisions that will create the consequences you would prefer as the vital healthy choice for your future life. Guaranteed! Like Jack LaLanne always said, *"Anything in life is possible, and YOU make it happen"*.

It is sad when we watch all of the commercials on television that portray someone needing to purchase this antacid or that pill to overcome the pain and suffering of the consequences of the junk people eat. In the developed world, there is no shortage of junk troughs to feed from in most every community. To make it worse, most people probably eat that junk in record time without chewing much of what they stuff down their throats! The manufacturer of the *acid-relief-to-the-rescue* produces the commercial with the tone that this poor being was a *victim* and can only be helped with the advertiser's products.

What has happened to both our sense of self-worth and common sense? I leave it up to you to decide what you should do. Personally, I have come to believe that the actual term *junk food* is an oxymoron. There is either junk – or there is food! You pick!

Vital Health Pillar Number 4 - Elimination: Oh, yuck! Do we have to talk about this? *Absolutely*! The first thing to discuss about the elimination of the waste we all create in our bodies is that, unfortunately, it's almost never discussed or even thought about, for that matter.

Bill Cosby toured the United States for a while doing a one-man show titled *Bill Cosby, Himself.* One of the segments, he did in that performance, was a parody of when a typical parent was trying to get a child *potty trained.* He painted a hilarious word picture of the child reluctantly sitting upon the *throne,* while the parent kneeled in front of the child, as Cosby says "*begging for it as if it were gold nuggets*"!

He went on to say that holding it back was the first time that the child discovered it had any real power. As funny as the scene was the first time I saw it, the humor is founded on truth.

Even though we all know this is a necessary and unavoidable bodily process, no one except medical professionals, or teenaged boys, want to *go there* in conversation. Despite its reputation for being one of the lowest, socially impolite, topics for discussion, nothing gets our attention faster, under any circumstance, than the need to purge our bodies of elements that just shouldn't be there any longer.

In the Health Pillar on Hydration, we have already covered enough about this one aspect of elimination and its vital function for our health and well-being. So, I won't spend any more time on it here. What we have not covered, however, are the vital activities and functions of what goes on in our stomach and the upper and lower intestines. Let's take a refresher look at what we're talking about:

According to medicinenet.com,

> *"The stomach is a muscular sac located on the left side of the upper abdomen. The stomach receives food"* (or junk, again, you pick) *"from the esophagus. As food reaches the end of the esophagus, it enters the stomach through a muscular valve called the lower esophageal sphincter. The stomach secretes acid and enzymes that digest food. Ridges of muscle tissue called rugae line*

the stomach. The stomach muscles contract periodically, churning food to enhance digestion. The pyloric sphincter is a muscular valve that opens to allow food to pass from the stomach to the small intestine.

The intestines are a long, continuous tube running from the stomach to the anus. Most absorption of nutrients and water happens in the intestines. The intestines include the small intestine, large intestine and rectum.

The small intestine (small bowel) is about 20 feet long and about an inch in diameter. Its job is to absorb most of the nutrients from what we eat and drink. Velvety tissue lines the small intestine, which is divided into the duodenum, jejunum and ileum.

What creates the velvety texture of the small intestine are very tiny hair-like filaments that line the intestines and capture whatever is trying to pass by on their way out of the system.

The large intestine (colon or large bowel) is about 5 feet long and about 3 inches in diameter. The colon absorbs water from wastes, creating stool. As stool enters the rectum, nerves there create the urge to defecate."

OK. Enough of the refresher class. Here is a critical point you may have never thought about. Those tiny little *hair-like* filaments, that "velvety lining" in the small intestine need cleansing. Without regular and very complete bowel movements, some very bad stuff begins to accumulate, harden and cause all kinds of problems. Our doctors don't even want to talk about this bad stuff, but it's *your bad stuff*, so you should give some thought to it.

There is a large and ever-growing group of professionals in the health and nutrition fields that believe that most disease starts here, in the middle of the *bad stuff* that is accumulating, sometimes for long, long periods of time, in your intestines. This accumulation of waste stuck in your gut becomes a toxic dump that then launches all sorts of disease throughout the rest of your body.

Again, I am just reporting as a researcher and not the expert here. But, the good news is that we live in the most incredible medical technology and information age in human history. Yet, people will religiously spend their time and hard earned money changing the oil and filters on their vehicles but won't spend five minutes looking into the health benefits of keeping their digestive system clean.

I have personally had family members become gravely ill and almost die from intestine-related issues that could have been managed with each of the points that have been shared with you in just the last few pages.

Here is a short list of specific steps you can control and use to balance your need for regular elimination of waste and toxins from your system:

1. Hydration (following Vital Health Pillar Number 2).

2. Daily aerobic exercise. Walking has long been referred to as a *constitutional* because it provides your body a healthy intestinal constitution.

3. Eat small frequent meals throughout each day (following Vital Health Pillar Number 5).

4. Maintain a balance of protein and carbohydrates, including multiple servings of fruits and vegetables, in your daily nutritional plan.

5. Eat in a relaxed state-of-mind.

6. Masticate completely.

7. Drink water (or other liquids) only before and no sooner than 10 minutes after eating solid foods. Consume a minimum of liquids during your meals to avoid flushing undigested food and nutrients through your system before they are broken down and assimilated.

8. Create a mindfulness and habit of more than one bowel movement during each day to minimize the amount of fermented food sludge you carry around with you.

So, now that you have done me, and yourself, the honor of reading this far, then "TAG, YOU'RE IT" for finding out how to make sure this is at least one very controllable area of your bodily function you can train yourself to operate vitally, cleanly and healthily!

Vital Health Pillar Number 5 - Aerobic and Anaerobic Training and Firing Up Your Metabolism: Re-read Chapter 5 and make a plan to which you will commit that will bring energized vitality and fitness into your future. Just remember, aerobic means with oxygen and anaerobic means without. Please don't just concentrate on one without the other.

> **me-ta-bo-lism n.** - *the chemical and physical processes continuously going on in living organisms and cells, including the changing of food into living tissue and the changing of living tissue into waste products and energy.* (Webster's New World Dictionary)

Here is the simplest and most straightforward way I think about this big word, *metabolism*. The quality, duration and effective vitality of changing processes from one to another is like combustion which, as you know, is the act of converting or burning one molecular structure into another form. An example would be converting wood to fire, vapor and smoke, and ultimately to heat. This is the way I visualize metabolism and maybe it will serve you.

Have you ever tried to keep a small fire going for a very long time, like all night? What do you think is the best way to keep a small fire burning hot and consistent all night?

Is it:

A. By continuously feeding it small to medium sized limbs? or,

B. By dropping the largest tree trunk-sized log you could carry on it and hope it lasts?

Your experience is showing if your answer is A. That's because you probably know if you drop the biggest tree trunk sized log on the fire all at once you would most likely smother and put the fire out.

Now take this simple analogy and apply it to what you eat, how often you eat, how you eat, how much you eat (size and portions) and when you eat it. Please take a sheet of paper and write down the answers to the following questions for you to use, one at a time, which would represent your typical consumption of food in a typical day:

- What do you eat?
- How often do you eat?

- How do you eat (here's a clue - look up "mastication")?
- How much do you eat in food sizes or portions?
- What times of day, or night, do you eat?

STOP ! DO NOT PROCEED WITHOUT COMPLETING YOUR ANSWERS !

Are you finished writing down as much as you can list about what you consume every day? If you did not do this process, I, of course, will never know it – but you will. If you have read this far, I thank you. However, this is not about me. This is about *you*. So, if you are too busy right now to do this, please place a bookmark here and come back when you can finish the process. This is very important for your future health!

What I find true for the fortunate (and smallest) percentage of us on the planet who are rich enough to have options of eating what and when we want, is we are operating on habits that go something like this:

- We eat a small, quick breakfast of convenience, if at all.
- We cram something down for lunch while remaining distracted in a busy mode so we rarely actually savor and enjoy chewing our food, usually *fast food*.
- We *snack break* on sugar, salted products and caffeine throughout the day.

(Your ticket to fat, higher blood pressure and an acidic system.)

- We get home in the evening tired and really hungry so we eat the largest meal of the day a couple of hours before bedtime.

Sound familiar? If your answer is yes, that's bad news for you! Now, think back to our small campfire analogy. The lesson, hopefully gleaned from this analogy, is that you should start each day by stirring up your *fire* (metabolism) with your training plan, then feed your *fire* all day long with small frequent, water saturated, fresh, uncooked foods that will keep the combustion of your metabolic system consistently burning all day long.

The result of employing the technique of eating small frequent meals is that you are not facing the daunting task of downing everything on a huge plate of food at each sitting. Further, you will develop the habit of giving yourself the gift of masticating your nutrients down to a level that your digestive system can become increasingly more efficient in burning them. Your energy will be consistently higher and the spells of feeling lethargic or hungry will be reduced.

If you have your lightest meal in the evening, your system will reward you by easily processing all of the other great decisions of what, when and how you ingested clean and nutritious foods throughout the day. The process converts your aggregate consumption into the energy and nutrition that your body needs. This will be accomplished overnight in a harmless and healthful way while you sleep. Your future health is built on the small decisions you make every day.

There is an old saying that goes, "We should all eat breakfast like a king or queen, lunch like a prince or princess and dinner like a pauper". I agree with the descending order of the volume of what is eaten that is described in that old saying. But, personally, I like the healthy and powerful feeling of keeping my combustion and metabolism cleanly and consistently burning and glowing all day long. If you ever come to one of my live seminars, you will discover I also treasure the *feeling* of high energy, vitality, aliveness and a positive expectancy that is born out of peak physical fitness and vital health. You will too!

CHAPTER 7
THE EMOTIONAL CORD

"Happiness is when what you think, what you say and what you do are in harmony."

– **Mahatma Gandhi**

The latter part of the 19th Century and throughout the early half of the 20th Century was an extremely prolific time for philosophers, journalists, medical doctors and psychologists to write, lecture and consult with their fellow beings. The explosion of publishing houses and breakthroughs in mass book printing and publishing was the equivalent of the "Information Age" of their day.

Some wrote of achieving financial wealth, others emotional health, others spiritual well-being and some wrote about the concept of *success* in any form. Regardless, each writer drew their inspiration from ancient philosophical, religious and spiritual teachings, their education, meditation and the lessons of their own lives and experiences.

Inspired by robust expansion and achievements of the *industrial age,* some began using bold phrases that their book contained the "*secrets* that can change your life", as stated on the back of the original printing of *Think and Grow Rich* by Napoleon Hill. It was the beginning of the *human potential movement.* Remember that the authors and lecturers were on different continents without the modern information sharing tools we enjoy today and came at their work from completely different backgrounds, education and experiences. And, yet, they each kept coming to the same order of Law in the Universe that they believed in and wrote about. Their writing turned out to possess common themes.

I became a student in the search of my own human potential, meaning and enlightenment in the 1960's with the purchase of two paperback books. One was the iconic book, *Think and Grow Rich*, by Napoleon Hill (I still own the original copy that I purchased for $.95 in 1964). The other was *Psycho-Cybernetics* by Maxwell Maltz, M.D. These two books seeded an appetite within me.

As I continued to purchase the works of others, some of the most influential included *As a Man Thinketh* by James Allen and *Man's Search for Meaning* by Dr. Viktor E. Frankl. I have since invested in my journey of enlightenment with many other books, seminars, tapes, CD's, and workshops.

I also studied the entire cassette tape series by Paul J. Meyer at Success Motivation Institute and completed Life Mastery University with Tony Robbins. Both of these experiences had a profound impact on me. But, it was those early books I have listed that set me on my path as a life-long seeker.

Even after the passage of 47+ years since the beginning of my journey of understanding and discovery, I continue to be amazed and grateful for the comfort and knowledge that I have gained from the consistency and uniformity of the messages that each of these authors teach in their writings. Their works are even more worthy of note in light of their disparate backgrounds.

So, what do all of these past writings have to do with your emotional well-being?

Simply put – possibly everything!

The human brain is, of course, the anatomical organ that produces all of the amazing functions and activity we discussed in Chapter 4. But, where exactly is the *mind* which we count on for our thoughts, feelings and our emotions?

There is a somewhat humorous and thought provoking story of the student who asked his Zen master, "Where is the mind"? The Zen master took a stone and used it to strike the student's toe, and then asked the student, "Where is your mind now"?

The use of the word "mind" has many meanings and uses in different languages. In addition to being the seat of consciousness for thoughts, memory and feelings, *mind* can also be defined to mean, to pay attention to; or one *minds*, or to care about (e.g., Yes, I mind; or no, I don't mind). There is even a well-worn phrase that claims *mind over matter*. But, in this chapter on your Emotional Cord, let's focus on *mind over emotions*.

Joseph Campbell (1904 - 1987) was a prolific American author, philosopher and teacher. He has also become one of the most quoted writers in American history. What he says about the question of the relationship between the mind and our emotions is certainly worthy of our consideration.

He said, *"The way to find out about happiness is to keep your mind on those moments when you feel most happy, when you are really happy — not excited, not just thrilled, but deeply happy. This requires a little bit of self-analysis. What is it that makes you happy? Stay with it, no matter what people tell you. This is what is called following your bliss"*.

Then Mr. Campbell went on to provide us with two more very powerful life impacting quotes:

"Find your bliss and the universe will open its doors for you where there were only walls."

and

"Your life is the fruit of your own doing. You have no one to blame but yourself."

The understanding that our emotions are an extension of our thoughts and our thoughts are created and spring forth from our minds is something to be reckoned with for all of us. Does finding your bliss mean bad things would never happen to us? Does it mean we can't be fooled or tricked by others, no matter if they are family, friend or foe? Of course not! Of adults, 100 percent are able to be tricked. But, healing and moving on is something we can learn and control.

It all begins with what I like to call our *spiritual self-image*. The discovery of and teaching of the term *self image* is something many psychologists and philosophers believe to be one of the most important discoveries of the 20th Century. The *self image* is believed to be a person's conceptual identity. It is simply what we believe to be true about ourselves.

Both our emotional state, as well as our behavior is designed to *prove* what we believe to be true, not to *disprove* it. This is true unless you possess some extreme neurosis in which your belief system and your behavior are not being reconciled. What we believe to be true about ourselves is based upon many factors, but, primarily it comes from the dominating thoughts that occupy our minds. The next question is *who chooses our thoughts*? The answer is, of course, we do!

Therefore, we can join our *self-image* to the spiritual aspect of our conceptual identity and, through this awareness, we can choose the thoughts that dominate our minds from that conceptual identity. We then begin to get a glimpse of the state of consciousness that is the *mind* from which our thoughts are given birth. But, no matter how many attempts are made to define how we humans operate, the fundamental origin of all achievement and growth is our willingness to risk believing it is possible for us to connect to the *creative universal energy* that all things share.

There are many in the various sciences today who believe genetic pre-disposition is the causal source for human behavior. This notion is one among biological and other motivations for the explosion in genetic research of the last several decades. However, newer studies are beginning to support the findings that genetic pre-disposition is only one, and often a minor factor in how humans behave and operate. What seems to have an even greater impact is the environment in which a person was raised and their willingness to accept their accountability for their personal power of choice.

Dr. Maxwell Maltz (1889 - 1975) was a plastic surgeon. In his practice he often experienced the opportunity to cosmetically transform the appearance of people who had suffered disfiguring physical trauma. Most of his patients were anxious, not only to get back to looking like they did before the trauma, they would also express their desire to get their life and relationships *back to normal* as a by-product of the surgery. However, what he discovered, as often as not, was the thought habits which developed during the period when the patient felt the most disfigured, survived the corrective surgery and their *self-image* didn't improve as hoped.

Years of similar outcomes with plastic surgery patients led Dr. Maltz to study and write *Psycho-Cybernetics* in 1960. His conclusion was that we are each a *goal-striving* mechanism. The goals we strive for are based upon our self-image. He determined the self-image can be changed and, in fact, a patient would more likely come closer to getting his or her life back to *normal* through the development of their *self-image*, than through corrective surgery alone.

Dr. Maltz's work is worthy of your reading to find ways to create your own emotional *facelift* through the building of your *self-image*. And, again, you can actually *decide* to make it happen. So how can your *self-image* be shaped by a simple act of deciding? My years of study have brought me to this firm conclusion:

Your ability to create a thought, and then risk using that thought to create an outcome, is the igniting spark of its realization.

It is this distinction which, among other unique attributes, makes human beings so blessed among all of the creatures of the world. So when it comes to finding, developing and nurturing the Emotional Cord of your parachute, you must first understand the inescapable consequences of the process born out of your choices to believe in your ability to risk the thought – just because it's there – rather than talking yourself out of the thoughts your creative mind gifts to you.

Many people find it easy to make excuses for why they can't, or shouldn't, try anything new.

When you think about what you would need to tackle a new idea or effort, what do you think you would need to start with?

When I ask this question in groups, I often get the response, "Confidence, that's what I need first". Then I ask, "Where does confidence come from?"

Look at the chart in Figure 6 and mentally think through the process with "A" as the starting point and work your way around the cycle. Creating a thought of what you want to do, and then being willing to risk doing it, is truly the starting point of all new endeavors. And, as your experience and confidence stretch and you build up your willingness to risk trying even more endeavors, the result is *growth*.

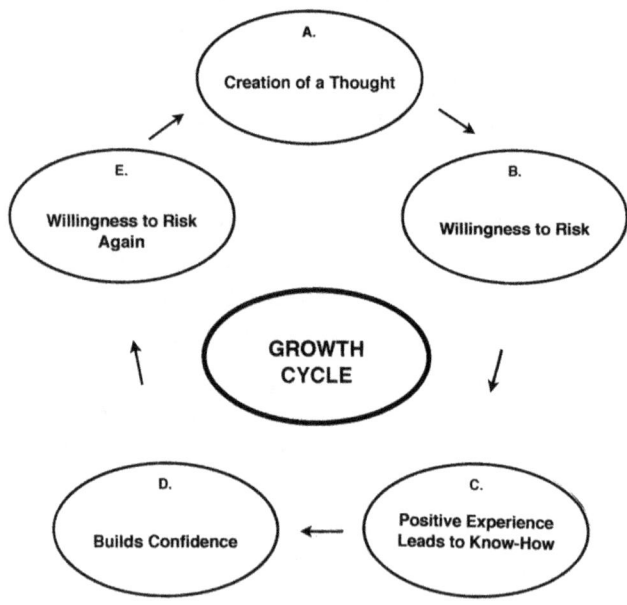

Fig. 6 - Rethink Age Institute Cycle of Thought Creating Growth from Interpretation of Choices

This Growth Cycle, which we teach at RethinkAge Institute, grows your ability to believe in yourself and build confidence from the experiences that you are willing to risk. It also builds your *self-image* and can lead to exploration of your potential. One of my favorite authors and philosophers, James Allen, has another way of putting the definition of this Growth Cycle into perspective.

James Allen (1864 - 1912) was a philosopher and author in England who had a writing career of only nine years prior to his death as a relatively young man at age 48. Despite his short writing career, he published 19 books that have had a lasting impact on humanity.

The second of his books was *As A Man Thinketh*, a title inspired by teachings from the Bible. His simple book is a literal primer on how to achieve emotional well-being. The significance of his book was due to the truths recognized by his readers, even though Allen, himself, failed to see its real value. His wife, Lily, had to convince him to publish it. Here are a couple of the relevant verses which provide the fundamental framework for who we become and what we achieve emotionally:

> *"Every man is where he is by the law of his being. The thoughts which he has built into his character have brought him there, and in the arrangement of his life there is no element of chance. All is the result of a law which cannot err. This is just as true of those who feel 'out of harmony'*

> with their surroundings as of those who are contented with them."

Today, as well as in James Allen's era, so many people in different societies try to blame circumstances for whatever emotional or other conditions in which they find themselves. Allen's position was very clear about the source of our circumstances and he provides us with a powerful perspective on the subject:

> *"Man is buffeted by circumstances so long as he believes himself to be the pawn of outside conditions. But when he realizes that he is a creative power, and that he may command the hidden soil and seeds of his being out of which circumstances grow, he then becomes his own master.*
>
> *Every man who has for any length of time practiced self-control and self-purification knows that circumstances grow out of thought. He will have noticed that the alteration in the circumstances has been an exact ratio with his altered mental condition. So true is this that when man earnestly applies himself to remedy the defects in his character, and makes swift and marked progress, he passes rapidly through a succession of changes.*

The soul attracts that which it secretly harbors; that which it loves, and also that which it fears. The soul reaches the height of its cherished aspirations; it falls to the level of its unchastened desires – and circumstances are the means by which it receives its own.

Every thought-seed sewn or allowed to fall into the mind, and to take root there, produces its own blossoming, sooner or later, into action and bearing its own fruit of opportunity and circumstance."

James Allen believed each of us has the ability to control our thoughts. He also believed that when we do control our thoughts we can control our emotions, and in so doing, master our circumstances. He believed this to be a Universal Law that was absolute and applied to all humans. He was also convinced and taught that the mind not only controls emotional health, but also controls our physical health. One additional quote from Allen's second book states:

"There is no physician like cheerful thought for dissipating the ills of the body; there is no comforter to compare with good will for dispersing the shadows of grief and sorrow. To live continually in thoughts of ill will, cynicism, suspicion and envy is to be confined in a self-made prison cell.

But, to think well of all, to be cheerful with all, to patiently learn to find good in all – such unselfish thoughts are the very portals of heaven."

What about when events beyond our individual control do *fall* upon us, altering our circumstances? One of the most beneficial uses of Allen's writings and teachings was to aid in the emotional healing of the mental effects on the survivors of World War I. But as those young survivors were aging into their 40's, another World War occurred in Europe and Russia.

As you know, during the earliest years of the rise of Hitler's power, Jews from all over Europe were rounded up, or tracked down, and either executed on the spot or sent to and concentrated in various camps. Of the millions who were incarcerated, the vast majority did not survive.

Viktor E. Frankl (1905 - 1997) was among the relatively few who did survive. As a highly educated and respected Austrian Neurologist and Psychiatrist, as well as being Jewish, Dr. Frankl was easily targeted. In his book, *Man's Search for Meaning*, Frankl described all of the conditions and circumstances of the Nazi concentration camps. He wrote that the combined circumstances *"conspire(d) to make the prisoner lose his hold. All the familiar goals in life are snatched away. What alone remains is the 'last of human freedoms' – the ability to 'choose one's attitude in a given set of circumstances'."*

What a powerful message for those of us who have never had to endure such extremely horrific circumstances.

Dr. Frankl found his own strength, meaning and a sense of purpose that contributed to his survival in circumstances that most might consider unsurvivable. He did this by making it his *purpose* to study, document and learn from his curiosity about the human capacity to endure suffering and find purpose or meaning in the daily struggle for existence in the camps. He wanted to understand why, under the same brutal conditions that all prisoners faced every day, some would simply give up and die overnight. Others, he observed, including himself, would continue with their will to survive, knowing of the horrors, or possibly even death, which would be waiting for them the next day.

What he discovered was that average humans have the capacity to endure senseless horrors and survive, as long as they choose to do so by focusing on a *purpose* that allowed them to rise above their outward fate. And, it didn't matter what that purpose might be, as long as the purpose held significant emotional meaning for that individual.

Once again, we are provided with an emotional life-lesson from the insights discovered and shared by others. Fortunately, you do not have to live through what Dr. Frankl did to learn from his experience. You only need to study from these masters like Maltz, Allen and Frankl to find your own truth in the application of what you seek in the form of emotional well-being.

Much of psychotherapy taught in the past, certainly prior to Dr. Frankl's experiences, was based upon analyzing what root causes existed in the patient's past that could explain their present day feelings and behavior. Dr. Frankl's observations, documentations and personal experiences set him upon a new school of psychotherapy which he named *logotherapy (logos* is the Greek word for *meaning*).

Frankl's explanation of *logotherapy* was that it was less retrospective than psychoanalysis in that it focused more upon introspection and the future. He placed great emphasis on the patient finding meaning within him or herself and using this strength to set a compelling future that would fuel his or her will to actualize that future.

I would also like for you to explore a possible parallel between the plasticity of the brain we discussed and how using the concepts taught by these authors could represent *emotional plasticity*. The proven ability of humans to choose their thoughts and thereby determine their behavior and outcomes certainly suggests that *emotional plasticity* is possible for all of us.

To be sure, this is an over-simplification of what *logotherapy* is all about. However, even in its simplest definition, it is my hope that you will connect with the value it can represent for you in finding your own emotional well-being by focusing on your own sense of purpose and meaning.

Examples of what is meant by this can be found in a more contemporary book by my friend, author, speaker and psychologist by the name of Dr. Elizabeth Lombardo. Dr. L, as she is fondly called, wrote a book titled *A Happy You*. You can check it out at www.ahappyyou.com.

"Effectively coping with stress is a skill, just like playing golf," says Dr. L. *"Some people are naturals, while most of us need training. But, you* can *learn. You* can *have less stress and greater happiness in your life, regardless of what is happening in your life. You just need to get the necessary tools. And, the more you practice them, the easier and more effective they become."*

In *A Happy You*, Dr. L provides chapter after chapter of those "necessary tools" that reduce stress and create emotional well-being. One of the many tools she recommends is exercise.

Although we covered physical fitness training extensively in Chapter 5, here are some bonuses from Dr. L that may help provide you with even more motivation to get off the bench and into your training plan. Did you know that exercise is good for your psychological health? Studies have shown that exercise:

- Raises mood-enhancing neurotransmitters in the brain
- Enhances positive attitudes
- Releases muscle tension
- Promotes better sleep

- Has a calming effect
- Lessens anxiety and depression

If you study Olympic athletes, you will find that they, too, rely heavily on achieving emotional balance through their training and exercise plan. We can *"wake up wonderfully"*, totally committed to the healthful and mind-enriching routines of training that we are committed to experience that day. The natural outcome *is* a feeling of emotional well-being and a positive attitude. Feeling that you have the power of choice to start each day *knowing* you are about to experience a *spirit, mind and body* enhancement will perform miracles for your emotional well-being.

Compare this to the way you may have awakened in the past or possibly even this morning. You can choose to *Wake up Wonderfully* not just some of the time, but every day for the rest of your life! It really is possible, and it is up to you.

Exercise is one of the many *fuels* that you can use to tune up your emotional well-being. Your car needs the proper fuel to get up to the *miles per hour* (MPH) that you demand. But, what I want to examine with you about the Emotional Cord of your parachute is this question: What kind of fuel can you create within you to experience the most *Smiles Per Hour* (SPH)?

What I know to be true is:

No matter what has happened in your past, you can *choose* the fuel to create more SPH in the future.

Another friend and contemporary psychologist who has taught me about creating fuel and tools for emotional well-being is Dr. Joan Rosenberg. Dr. Rosenberg is a clinical psychologist who has worked at UCLA, USC and is currently an Adjunct Professor of Psychology at Pepperdine University in Los Angeles. Dr. Rosenberg has a very useful tool to help you find your emotional balance and well-being. Using a memory trigger from Albert Einstein's famous formula, Dr. Rosenberg invited me to share her formula with you which is "$E = mc^4$". Her explanation as to how we can use this formula is:

Emotional Vitality and Well-being = **Meaning** derived from "**C's**" to the **fourth** power:

1. **Connection** - your capacity to acknowledge, accept and trust your everyday emotional experiences.

2. **Congruence** - when your words and actions match your thoughts and feelings, you feel present and fully alive. Connection and congruence also help you establish community.

3. **Community** - your connection with others; combined with the two elements above lead to Contribution.

4. **Contribution** - offering your skills, knowledge, time, support and perspective to

others actualizes your service. This contribution leads to a feeling that you are living a life filled with purpose and meaning.

The key to a beneficial application of Dr. Rosenberg's formula is your *awareness* of how you have chosen to weave the four C's into your daily life with your self-image, sense of meaning and purpose. It is a simple formula. But, when it is applied in the form of questions on a daily basis, it can bring us ever closer to the emotional balance that all of us seek as a fully-functioning and fulfilled human being. To learn more about the work of Dr. Rosenberg, which she calls *Emotional Pilates*, visit her website at emotionalpilates.com.

In our examination of the influence of thoughts on our emotional well-being, we would be remiss not to distinguish the differences and consequences of two expressions of our thoughts. The two are, a) thoughts we think in our brains and choose not to express outwardly; and, b) thoughts we express outside to the world in written or language forms.

A very old and accepted quote is "the pen is mightier than the sword". The truth and significance of this saying needs no explanation to anyone who has studied history. It is also another way of stating that language, and specifically our words, have great power.

Think, for a moment, of all of the religious and political leaders, philosophers, teachers, authors, songwriters and poets who have influenced humans with their words throughout history. In a matter of just a few minutes, you could create an impressive list of the most influential women and men who have literally shaped the affairs and destiny of humanity with just their words. In all aspects of our lives, words have the power to build or tear down, to create or destroy, to connect or disconnect and to inspire or discourage.

Here are some seriously important questions that will have a direct impact on you and those with whom you come into contact that deserve equally serious and thoughtful answers from you. Please open up your personal journal and document how you are relating with yourself and others using your words. This is a simple and quick process that will pay huge dividends immediately. Do the process as if the future function of your Emotional Cord depended upon it! (HINT: Don't analyze as you write, just let yourself go and write freely. You can edit later.)

1. What are the descriptive words that you use on a habitual basis?

2. What are the origins of the words you use in your daily life?

3. Have you taken any account of how the words you habitually use affect or reinforce your attitudes and self-image?

4. What words do you use most often that express your self-image?

5. What effect do the words you normally use have on those around you?

6. What words do you want to begin developing into your language habits that will help you achieve the emotional balance you desire?

The search tool on quotefinder.org produced the following anonymous quote which illustrates the power of the thoughts into which we breathe life in the form of words:

"Watch your thoughts, for they become words.

Watch your words, for they become actions.

Watch your actions, for they become habits.

Watch your habits, for they become character.

Watch your character, for it becomes your destiny."

Every emotion is associated with a corresponding feeling in your physical body. I am certain you have had a feeling in your mind that you were being followed or watched, and that feeling turned into other emotions such as fear, annoyance or curiosity. As you acknowledge this very real feeling in your physical body, you then take some notice or action, only to discover that you were being neither watched nor followed.

Your feelings do not judge or apply the level of value on whether the thoughts are negative or positive, angry or joyful, sad or happy. Every experience you *feel* is the manifestation of the thoughts you hold in your mind. As these feelings register within us, it is important to realize your mind does not know the difference between a real or imagined experience. This is a very powerful piece of information to hold in your awareness. The *real* power comes in the form of using this knowledge to control the emotion that would normally come from the experience.

As poignant as the examples in Dr. Frankl's concentration camp scenarios were, history is filled with many examples of humans who have suffered unfair or even horribly unthinkable experiences. How they chose to interpret and apply those experiences determined their emotional well-being in their individual futures.

Who comes to mind for you as examples of how the spirit and mind of a human being can thrive beyond negative or even painful experiences? Maybe you are your own best example.

We are very good at discounting the progress we make in these matters. Sometimes we are so good at putting a negative or painful experience behind us that we don't have to deal with it. We forget that it was our own will and processing that pulled us through and helped us heal ourselves.

The ability of the human to process and heal, especially related to our emotions, is yet another gift of being human that deserves our attention. If you can get past a negative or painful experience once, you can repeat that process anytime in the future. This is truly a unique characteristic of being human for which we can be grateful.

Gratitude is another interesting topic. It has a healing and emotional well-being power component to it. Gratitude adds to the positive energy in the universe and builds positive connections between you and all the things for which you are grateful. It is like an emotional magnet that draws positive energy, relationships and outcomes into your life.

If you like the concept of adding more SPH to your everyday experiences, one of the surest ways to get there is to choose an *attitude of gratitude* as a part of your self-image. Make an *attitude of gratitude* something that you count on for yourself and also are known for among those with whom you come into contact on a daily basis, whether friend, acquaintance or stranger. Gratitude is the high octane booster to get those increases in SPH's and just feel better each day. Again, it's your choice!

The last area for you to consider is one that may seem obvious, but is also taken for granted. That is your environment. The accumulation of clutter and its impact on your emotional well-being is something worth considering. You may be like me and become depressed when we allow our environment to become cluttered and disorganized. I think if you are truly honest with yourself you know what I mean. If you have ever participated in a yard or garage sale, you know *exactly* what I mean.

On this subject, I want to refer you to an expert named Lorie Marrero. Check out her website www.clutterdiet.com. This is an amazing resource that provides a whole world of ideas and tips on how to simplify your life. As a result of the information and systems offered there, you can clean up your environment and reduce your stress. I highly recommend it.

Of course, there are many other elements in your environment besides clutter that have an impact on your emotional well-being. The primary message here is for you to carefully examine what factors are making you unhappy on a reoccurring basis and what factors are making you happy on a reoccurring basis. Awareness allows you to be your own best advocate, and it can help you create the emotionally balanced life you want.

Your choices about your emotional balance will have a tremendous impact on your relationships – which we talk about NEXT!

CHAPTER 8
THE RELATIONSHIPS CORD

"Kindness is more important than wisdom, and the recognition of this is the beginning of wisdom."

- Theodore Isaac Rubin

Obviously, it only takes any one cord of our parachute to get tangled up with some sort of knot in it to create dysfunction in our "flight" through life. But, one of the cords that seem to be continually getting knots in it is in the Relationship Cord.

Let's take a careful examination of what elements are woven together that seem to create this frequent tendency for dysfunction. We will do this by, first, understanding that the relationships in our lives come in three primary areas.

One is our relationship with ourselves. That's right, we must examine how we feel about and treat ourselves as a starting point to understanding how we relate to and treat others. Then we can focus on the second area which is our relationship with others. The third area is our relationship with the global community you now know as your Human Family.

Nurturing Your Self-Relationship

Most of us are born into this world full of wonder and possibilities. We don't know anything is, or is not, possible. Our learning begins with our first breath. Although none of us remembers what thoughts were going on in our brains on that first day out of our mother's womb, it would be fun and interesting to imagine it.

"Wow, where am I?"; and, "How did I get here?"; and, "Who are all these people?"; and, "Why am I so cold?"; and, "Why is it so bright and loud here?"; and, "Getting here sure made me tired!" and, "What's for dinner?" If I am that baby, the first order of business is finding ways to get all of *my* needs satisfied. In this early stage of human life, I don't know, nor do I care, about the complexities of relationships with others.

It doesn't take very long to realize, however, that if I begin to acknowledge and foster a relationship with these others around me, not only do my needs get met, I begin to feel loved and they all seem pretty happy as well. So we begin to learn the value of thinking, "OK, here's another cute smile for the big person that's holding me."

Thus begins a life-long experimental journey of finding out about the relationship complexities and the balancing act of *my* needs versus *their* needs. Through this life-long process of understanding our own existence, and doing so in the light of relating and balancing needs, we begin to make decisions about what works and what does not work.

In our formative years through early adulthood, all of these judgments of what works, or doesn't work, must pass through the filter of its impact on the self, first. In other words, does it work *for me*, or not? And, thus grows the deeply rooted perspective from which most people operate, which is living their lives tuned into only one FM station. That station is WII-FM, which stands for What's In It For Me? Considering what was going on for most of us as babies, it is understandable how this perspective was originated.

Our relationship with ourselves is every bit as challenging as our relationship with others. Yet, we are presented with a fascinating enigma. Have you noticed that most of us will demand of ourselves much more than we would demand of others? And, yet, have you observed that we insist others take care of themselves while we do not take care of ourselves as well? Is it common that you will not block out the uninterrupted time you need to accomplish the things you wish to accomplish? But, you would never think about breaking an appointment with someone else nor would you be comfortable interrupting others if they said they were too busy to be with you at a particular moment.

And, so, the enigma; why is it that so many of us have a WII-FM orientation but, then, put ourselves last on the list of what we know would make our personal parachute fly true, far and with less effort?

The answer may lie in *bugs*. Yes, I did say *bugs*.

You probably have experienced *bugs* or *software glitches* in your computer. Well, as wonderful and fortunate as we humans are, we also come with *bugs* in our *operating software*. We know *all* software doesn't have *bugs* and, so it is with humans. We don't all have the same *bugs* but most of us do have some. Most psychologists agree there are at least three very common *bugs* in the software many humans seem to share. These human software *bugs* are:

    Am I good enough?

      Am I lovable?

       Am I worthy?

Most of us achieve some satisfaction in sorting out the questions of these human software *bugs* early in life. But, what each of us learns about the answers to each of these questions will be reflected in our level of self esteem, translate into our self-image and sculpt our relationship with ourselves and others.

As we have discussed in previous chapters, the good news is we can harness our power of choice to be able to answer and deal with these *bugs* at any point in our lives, simply by embracing our connection with the *creative universe* and acknowledging what amazingly wonderful creatures we are. From this connection and acknowledgement, we can then choose to repair our software. This repair happens when we replace bugs of doubt with three other, more accurate, beliefs. They are:

> I am uniquely priceless!
>
> I am certainly lovable!
>
> I am naturally worthy!

Most people on the planet do not understand, or use, this amazing *power of choice* over what we think, say or do. This power of choice allows us to repair our own *bugs*. When you use this powerful gift, you can nurture and develop your relationship with yourself. To do so will ultimately reflect outwardly how you nurture and develop your relationship with others. It is sheer folly to expect that you can operate with a negative relationship with yourself and have a wholesome and positive relationship with others.

If you have doubts about this, take another look at Dr. Joan Rosenberg's formula "$E=mc^4$", in Chapter 7, and, think again. This formula applies equally well to the understanding and development of relationships as it does in creating emotional well-being.

Now, about those relationships with others. As I was growing up and going through my own understanding of my human operating software, early programming by my parents taught me many different foundational rules of *getting along* with others. Examples were to always say "please" and "thank you", trust people, be kind and thoughtful, always open the doors for girls and women to enter first, respect my elders, don't hit my brother, "love thy neighbor as thyself", and a few hundred more relationship techniques.

But, somewhere early on, as I entered school, so many other people didn't seem to be so kind, loving or considerate to me. So, like most kids, I began to build my protective armor. This armor-building really worked! Stay quiet, in some circumstances, and don't get involved was a good plate of protection. Being funny and silly to win approval and deflect attention to those dreaded personal software *bugs* added yet another plate to my armor. There were other techniques, but you get the idea, and I am sure you can relate.

Over the years I became pretty good at adding to and using my armor. The older I got, and the more I experienced life, the more my armor came in handy. I strengthened it with each passage in my early adulthood; in the army, in college, as a young husband, in each job I started and as a father. The forging and hardening of my armor went on and on.

As it became more and more perfected, I became a confident warrior in my business and professional life and nothing could get through my armor or to me. I seemed, however, to have more and more difficulty with my personal and family relationships.

One day, after two failed marriages, a disconnected long distance relationship with my two sons by my first marriage and no real friends that I could think of, I found myself alone in my super-perfected armor. "How could this be?" I asked myself. "I'm a nice guy. I'm still doing all those things my Mom and Dad taught me."

I re-read some of those books I mentioned in the previous chapter and I went through some serious introspection and retrospection. That is when I came upon a revelation. While my wonderfully impervious armor was keeping anything from getting through to me on the inside, it was just as perfectly keeping everything to which anyone could relate from getting to the outside. I had become a prisoner in my own armor and the rest of the world didn't particularly care whether I was locked up in there or not!

With this revelation fresh in my mind, I made the decision to relocate closer to my two sons. I stopped worrying about finding that "right woman". I also concentrated on and started peeling off my armor and getting a healthy relationship with *myself!*

I moved from where I was living in Arizona to Texas to be near the boys and, over the next year, began the process of finding my own peaceful center. As I continued to work on trying to rebuild a relationship with my sons and learn how to become more vulnerable without my armor, I also decided not to date or put any pressure on myself to find the right someone, just yet.

Then something quite wonderful and amazing happened. When I wasn't seeking or longing, I suddenly found the love of my life, Marilyn. Even more interesting, in that moment, was that she, also, had just about given up on dating and trying so hard to find the right someone. She, too, had decided to focus on getting balanced and centered within her own self. The conclusion that she didn't *need* someone else in her life besides her daughter, her family and friends was her turning point. Fortunately, it occurred in about the same time frame as when I chose to start making my big changes.

I had been talking to her on the phone through business calls to her boss (she was the "gatekeeper" for him) for nearly a year, but we had never met in person. One day I popped off and said, "My New Year's resolution is that we should meet". She agreed and so we arranged a *blind date* with each other. When I arrived at her home and she opened the door...Well, I *can* tell you that there *is* such a thing as love at first sight!

We were married seven months later. That was in 1983 and our marriage and relationship are getting better every day.

And I got a bonus! I instantly became the father of her 12 year old daughter who I love and cherish as my own. Also, Marilyn, my children, my grandchildren and all my friends are continuing to help me remove any remaining pieces of armor that would keep me from enjoying the emotional freedom I was gaining from this process. Life is good!

Building Relationships With Others

"Life is an echo; whatever you send out is what comes back."
- **Chinese Proverb**

For the Relationship Cord of our parachute to work for us every time, not just some of the time, we need to maintain a certain fundamental awareness and understanding of how critical it is to develop and maintain a healthy and positive relationship with ourselves first. This basis of the successful relationship-building process begins with what I call *The Law of Relationship Reciprocity*. The *Law* requires that you *be* what you want to *experience*. Examples of this *Law* are illustrated by the following axioms:

- To have more good people in your life – be good!

- To experience more love in your life – be more loving!

- To surround yourself with positive people – be more positive!

- To have more friends – be friendlier!

I could go on and on with these axioms but what matters to you are the axioms that reflect what you want to create in the relationships in your life. So, ask yourself, "What are the *echos* I want to experience back from what I put out?" Take a moment, right now, and make up your own list in your personal journal or on a separate piece of paper. Use the following framework for your relationship desires:

In order to _____ – I will be _____!

Repeat the formula above, creating your own personal axioms, until you have aligned what you want to create within yourself to what you want to attract from others.

The Beatles may have been the most successful singing group in history. I like nearly all of their music, but, I also appreciate most of the messages that they delivered within it.

In the *Abbey Road* album, The Beatles sang a tract titled "The End". The last verse in that song almost whispers, "*and in the end, the love you take, is equal to the love you make.*" What an interesting way to sing a restatement of the *Golden Rule*.

Women are generally very good at creating and maintaining close relationships with other women over long periods of time. My wife has two close girlfriends that date back over 5 decades. I do not share this distinction. I have learned this natural interest and attraction to connection with others is something most men do not share either.

The typical male does not naturally possess the same tendency to create very close long-term bonding relationships with other males. That is common in the males of most species. By searching insidefacebook.com, we can easily see women are also the majority users of Facebook rather than men. This is particularly true of Facebook users who are 35 years of age and older. An interesting trend, however, is among those in the 18 to 25-year old category where use by males exceeds females. One explanation could be that younger adult males are shopping for female relationships.

Overall, particularly among the large Baby Boomer segment of the population around the world, work demands, drive for competition and early programming have generally limited male interest in building close personal relationships with other male friends. Even the thought of not having many close male friends is not something that demands more than an occasional passing thought by most men that I know.

The *friends* they do have and with whom they share time through clubs, sports, and hobbies or on social media, do not have the same bonded connection and intensity that is fairly common in the relationships between women. However, the good news is that as we grow older, and hopefully wiser, men, like women, tend to seek and find closer friends when doing so becomes more of a priority.

Have you ever met someone, developed a casual acquaintanceship with them and then wondered why they never call you? On the other hand, have you invested in that relationship by calling them first?

Like most everything that has been written within the pages of this book, the number, quality, joy, length and frequency of contact of your relationships is also within your *power of choice*. If you are perfectly happy with these elements of your relationship with others, congratulations! But, if you seek more from your relationships, you know that this, too, is within your ability to take the necessary steps.

The Chinese are not the only ones with quotable proverbs. Where I was raised, we have "Texas Proverbs". One that seems appropriate here is, "You don't know the worth of water until the well goes dry". And, so it is true with, not just our relationships with those we know, but also within our entire Human Family.

The Global Relationships Connection

I am proud to have been a member of Rotary International for many years. Although there are many worthwhile service organizations around the world, the oldest, and in my experience, a most successful one, is Rotary International. Founded in 1905 in Chicago, Illinois, Rotary International now consists of 1.2 million members in 34,000 Rotary clubs located in over 200 countries. Rotary is a worldwide network of inspired individuals who translate their passions into relevant social causes to change lives in their communities. Rotary's men and women members around the world are dedicated to service, fellowship, diversity, integrity and leadership. These areas of focus, combined with Rotary's motto of "Service Above Self", form the foundational principals for the organization.

One additional area of emphasis on which Rotarians focus is the goal of international understanding, peace and goodwill. It has been one of the greatest privileges for Marilyn and me to join with other Rotarians from around the world to achieve those goals. Our opportunities have been played out in many different types of projects that have connected us with what I consider as our larger Human Family.

These connections have created a fundamental shift in my perspective about those billions of members of our Human Family whom I don't know personally and will never meet. Almost everyday we hear about something tragic that has happened on another part of our shared Planet.

Hardly a week goes by that I don't hear someone here in the U.S. saying something like, "Wow, that's terrible for those poor people. I wish there was something I could do, but, I'm just one person." What a perfect attitude to guarantee our isolation from each other.

Another common theme I hear from people in supposedly developed countries is, "We have enough problems here so why should we worry about anyone 'over there' whom we will never meet?"

That's a fair question and, by the example which follows, I would like to propose a fair answer for you to consider. Once you consider it, I encourage you to share those conclusions with those people you know.

The more enlightened and global Human Family view is the one taken by members of Rotary International, The Rotary Foundation and other similar global service organizations. In this view, even though one person cannot fix all of the problems and challenges in the world, there is practically no limit on the positive impact that touches millions, if not billions, of lives when we partner together for a worthy cause.

One of the best examples of global partnering for massive change of which I know of is the global war to eradicate the horrific disease of *polio* that Rotary International has been leading since 1985. If you are lucky, you may not even really know anything about the polio virus.

Poliomyelitis is a viral disease that can affect nerves and can lead to partial or full paralysis. When the paralysis attacks the muscles that control the diaphragm and lungs, the patient will suffocate and die unless they have access to an iron lung. There are still a few people in the world that have lived their entire lives in an iron lung.

There are millions of people who are permanently crippled from this disease. Also, there are also untold numbers of people who are dealing with on-going symptoms of the disease called "post-polio syndrome".

This war against the ravages of polio began as all revolutions do – as a single thought in the mind of one human being. In 1979, a Rotarian in the Philippines wanted to see the children on his island stop getting polio. He convinced his Rotary Club to apply for assistance from the Rotary Foundation. By matching a Rotary Foundation Grant with the funds raised by Rotarians on the island, they were able to inoculate each child on the island with just two tiny drops of oral vaccine. Within just one year, there were *no* new cases of polio on the island. After a visiting Rotary District Governor heard of this project and sent in his report, the leaders of The Rotary Foundation became focused and excited about the prospect of providing this same gift of life to all of the children of the world.

When Rotary International approached the World Health Organization (WHO), an arm of the United Nations, about what would be required to eliminate from the planet, a disease which had developed over thousands of years, their first reaction was that it couldn't be done. They had good reason for their position.

Prior to this goal of eradicating polio, there had been only one disease in history declared as eradicated by human effort by the WHO. That was smallpox in 1979. (More recently, Rinderpest was declared eradicated in 2010.) But, when Rotary committed both the money and the *volunteer army* of 1.2 million individual Rotarians around the world to support the actual immunization of all of the at-risk children in the world, an agreement was completed.

Rotary partners since this beginning have included UNICEF, the U.S. Centers for Disease Control (US-CDC), the governments of many nations and other non-profit foundations, the largest of which is the Bill and Melinda Gates Foundation and the on-going fund-raising and personal immunization efforts of individual Rotarians and others around the world. Although polio had almost completely disappeared in Europe, Japan and North America by the early 1960's, when the 1985 Rotary launch of the polio eradication campaign began, there still were over 150 polio endemic countries in the world who were collectively suffering hundreds of thousands of new cases per year.

Today, Rotarians and their global partners have immunized over two billion children in the world.

So, what about the results of this unprecedented quiet army of service minded partners? In the 25 years after Rotary started this campaign, in the entire year of 2010, there were only 1,292 new cases reported in the world. As of June 30, 2011, there were only 229 cases of polio reported in the world.

Obviously this has been a long and expensive battle. But, now a whole new generation of our Human Family will grow up to become productive members of our planet. Someday, the new generation will explain what polio *once was* to their children. This happened because of that single thought in the mind of *one* person. It took just one person to decide, not just *wish* things were different, but to decide to *act* on his thought!

What will that thought be for you? What connections will you make with a partner organization to make your thought become a reality?

When I was originally thinking about a title for this book, one option was "The Big Picture". I discovered this prospective title was being used too much so I abandoned it. I still believe, however, that it certainly is appropriate for the subject of our relationship with our other human inhabitants of the Earth.

Early on in this book, I shared information about how all creatures are connected and part of the same Universal Energy. Hopefully this makes intuitive, if not outright sense to you. Within this unlimited field of energy, the suffering of one has a real, though subtle, impact on all other beings.

Our societies have become so materially, physically and *self-oriented* (remember WII-FM?)that this may seem like a very esoteric and abstract concept. When one person suffers, or even dies, it doesn't seem to physically affect you or materially deprive you, unless you know them or you are related to them personally. So how could it be that there is any connection at all?

Let's use the example of a neighborhood within a community or village. In this neighborhood, pretend you have an individual home you treasure and attend to constantly. Both your home and its grounds are immaculately cared for and beautiful. However, all of the other homes in the neighborhood are in various conditions of decay, lawns are overgrown with weeds and covered in trash. There has been an outbreak of graffiti and broken windows on the exterior of those *other* homes in your neighborhood. You have watched this decay evolve over a period of time and wished it was not this way. You have even noticed this same decay is starting to show up throughout your entire community. But, you kept thinking to yourself, "It's not my place to say or do anything about this, and, after all, what can one person do?" So you did nothing.

Eventually, you feel that this is not the neighborhood or community in which you want to live for the rest of your life. So, you decide you will sell your beautiful home. You contact a realtor who tells you your home is now the best home in town. First, however, you must get your immaculate home appraised to determine its value and what the sales listing price should be.

You can guess what happens next, right? Yes, the appraiser is very complimentary about your home. Then the appraiser informs you that since the value of your home is based on the *comparable* values to the homes in your neighborhood, your home will not bring much of a price at all, despite all of the attention you have paid to it alone.

In the world of relationships, we all live in a global community that is divided into neighborhoods. You and I represent just one individual home in our global community. This is an analogy of what happens when one's total focus is only on themselves without recognizing the consequence of disregarding the surrounding *neighborhoods* of our Human Family.

One of my favorite stories that illustrates the power, importance and difference one person can make in global influence is a parable told by Rajendra K. Saboo, from Chandigarh, India, the 1991-92 President of Rotary International. Rajendra told a story of the wealthiest man in a country who was faced with choosing which of his two sons would run his empire when he was no longer able. After giving the issue much thought, he called his two sons to his side to reveal the plan he had devised. He explained that each son would receive the same small amount of gold in a leather bag. Their challenge was to go out into the world and trade the gold for something they could bring back to fill up every room of their vast castle. Each boy agreed and began their journey the next morning.

After weeks had passed, the first son returned with a long caravan of oxen pulling carts. Each cart was piled high with straw. Upon arrival the father and his staff greeted the boy and they proceeded to cover the floor of each room with the straw until it was finished. The father was pleased with his son's completion of the task and congratulated him.

Before the next week passed, the second son arrived with only a wooden yoke across his shoulders. Hanging on each end of the yoke were large cloth bags which bulged with something the father, the brother and their staff could not see. After offering the proper greeting to his father and brother, the second boy unfolded his bags and began to take candles to each room and filled the castle with light.

We don't have to solve all of the problems of the world. But imagine what could happen if each of us just lit our one candle. Imagine if each of us paused our busy lives of inward focus and somehow managed to agree to light six billion individual candles in support of each other in our Human Family. Imagine a world filled with the light of global community relationships!

Whether your focus on relationships is with yourself, others who are closely around you or is in relating to your global Human Family, the quality of all your relationships will be determined by the questions you ask of yourself. It is up to you to determine the type and quality of relationships you want to maintain for your own sense of fulfillment.

If you seek to actively change your relationships, the starting point is for you to consciously determine, through self-questioning, what that change means to you. You don't have to accept your current relationships or condition in any area of your life. However, that which we don't refuse to accept tends to become an agreement, whether it is about relationships or any other condition of our existence. If you find yourself feeling like you want to improve the Relationships Cord of your parachute, remember this simple phrase:

What you seek you will find and what you put out there will come back to you, often in multiples of what you put into it!

CHAPTER 9
THE FINANCIAL CORD

"What the mind of man can conceive and believe, it can achieve."

- Napoleon Hill

One day in 1908, twenty-five year old Napoleon Hill (1883 - 1970) was meeting with industrialist, businessman, entrepreneur and philanthropist, Andrew Carnegie (1835 - 1919). Carnegie was born of humble origin in Dunfermline, Scotland, to a woman who was a weaver. When he was a child, Carnegie and his parents migrated to the United States. His first job, as a young boy in the United States was as a worker in a factory making bobbin spools for thread. Later he became a billing clerk for the owner of the company. He eventually became a messenger.

As he got older, he went to work for a telegraph company where he progressed up the ranks quickly. Over the years that followed, he made a special effort to learn and excel at everything he attempted in telegraphy, railroads, bridge building and other industries.

He created Carnegie Steel Company in the 1870's and grew the company until its sale to J.P. Morgan in 1901 as U.S. Steel. After the sale, at seventy-three years of age, Carnegie was considered the second wealthiest man in America, next to John D. Rockefeller, and one of the most powerful men on earth.

Napoleon Hill was also not born into privilege. This meeting and its setting in Carnegie's office was in stark contrast with the small rural town in Virginia where Hill was born. That little mountain town did not hold much promise for young Hill in the late 1800's. His mother died in 1893 and just two years later, he became a freelance reporter, working for a small town newspaper, writing for pennies per line at the age of 13.

Imagine what it must have felt like, just 12 years later, when Hill was in Carnegie's office. He managed to get this interview because he had received an assignment to write a series of articles about men who were both famous and financially successful during that period of time. Fortunately, Andrew Carnegie had developed a "success formula", in an outline form, based upon his own results. He believed his formula could be used by anyone to achieve success and he wanted to talk about it to someone who would take it to the public.

As Carnegie discussed his success formula with Hill, he saw something special in the young journalist. So Carnegie decided to offer the Hill a chance to take on the task of spending the next 20 years studying 500 successful people. As a part of this assignment, Hill was to also apply the Carnegie formula wherever he could to test the ability of the average person to be able to use it for his or her own success.

Hill's journey and work experience produced a multi-volume home study course for success initially published in 1925 called *The Law of Success*. Later, in 1937, Hill's writings turned into one of the best selling books of all time, *Think and Grow Rich*. Hill and Carnegie were anxious to share their secret to success and even envisioned a time when this secret would be taught in the school systems of the nation.

Napoleon Hill went on to become a lecturer, attorney and advisor to business executives and U.S. presidents. He authored several more books, teaching others how to achieve success in their lives. The work of Napoleon Hill taught many millions of people around the world those proven secrets about how to achieve the financial success of their dreams. One of the challenges he posed to his readers was for each to develop a definite major purpose by asking themselves, "In what do I truly believe"? This question is as valid today as it was when it was first pondered by Hill.

Despite the information, inspiration and success formula having been published and republished so long ago, the vast majority of people in the world approach their lives with an attitude of limitation and what I call a "poverty consciousness". According to Hill, 98 percent of people he worked with and surveyed had few or no firm *beliefs*. This fact alone certainly put meaningful success out of their reach. And yet, not surprisingly, most of those same people admitted they would really like to have a great deal more money and become financially independent.

If the same success formula that Carnegie used and Hill worked to communicate is clearly available, why is there such a disparity between those who have financial wealth and independence and those who do not? This is a huge and very complex question and one that deserves some investigation. By interviewing professional financial planners, I have learned how some of the disparity occurs and, more importantly, what any individual can do to correct it.

First, each of us would benefit from our own determination of how we, as adult humans, think about money and where our own personal "money philosophy" was originated. What follows is a great place to start your probe into your own money philosophy.

Pretend, for just a few minutes, you are in the office of a financial planner who is asking you to answer some questions that will help you discover your money philosophy. Please take a sheet of paper, or your journal, and write out the answers to the questions that follow. Write down as much detail as you can with each of your answers. This process will get your money philosophy out of your head and down on paper.

In just a few short minutes you will discover where your money philosophy came from, where it has taken you and what you can do to improve it. Here are the questions based upon several important elements of your money philosophy:

1. What is your first memory of money?
2. What were your family's regular discussions about money, if any?
3. What is your definition of money, or as I like to ask, what is your money perspective?
4. What is your definition of financial independence?
5. What does money have to do with your happiness?
6. How much wealth accumulation is a *must* for you?
7. When you achieve the wealth that is a *must* for you, how will your life be different?

8. What would you like to do for others with the additional money you can accumulate?

When you have invested some serious thought into your answers, you will have a much better understanding of how your money philosophy works. You can create the habits of thought that better represent what you want to achieve for your future.

One of the concepts that financial planners often seek to share with their clients is that *money is just a tool*. If you want to dig a hole, your best tool would be a shovel. If you want financial independence, money is the best tool to accomplish that.

If you found your family treated money "as the root of all evil", you have probably had some difficulties with attracting, and keeping, money. If the subject of money was not even part of the conversation in your family as you were growing up, it may be time to take a fresh look at what money is or can be for you. I hope this text may help you do that.

As we have discussed before, what happened in your past is important to acknowledge, but we cannot live in the past. We want to begin making our futures more in alignment with our highest hopes and wishes. It does not matter if your earliest memory about money was listening to arguments between your parents about not having enough; or always being told you could not have something you wanted because there was "just not enough money to go around".

You may have been asked, "Do you think that money just grows on trees"? It's important to understand you may be holding on to that as part of an attitude of scarcity that could be limiting your financial independence. You have the power and the ability to choose to think differently and change your attitude in the process.

There are many definitions of financial independence. But a great friend of mine, and the president of his own successful financial planning and securities firm, provided me with what I like to think is a good definition. He said, "When your life decisions do not have to revolve around money, you are financially independent".

This is a remarkably freeing definition! It does not have anything to do with how much money you have. It also has nothing to do with how much anyone else has by comparison, either. Unless you are *the* single richest person on Earth, someone else always has more money than you do. What this financial planner's definition addresses is the real issue of *feeling* financially independent, and, therefore, wealthy. It is how you feel about the money you have versus what you feel compelled to spend.

Have you noticed each time you may have had an increase in income that rarely translates into greater financial independence? Does the inclination to spend more when you make *more* sound familiar? Financial independence also has to do with having enough money for you to have peace of mind. If you are always spending as much or more than you are taking in, then obviously, peace of mind is going to be difficult to achieve. The great news is you can achieve peace of mind about money faster with a shift in your expectations of what you "have to have" than by simply trying to make more.

My financial planner friend tells me that typically, a woman who is newly widowed, and who may never have had a large sum of money before the death of her husband, spends her life insurance proceeds within an average of *three years*, regardless of how much money that may have been.

She is obviously in emotional pain from the loss of her loved one. To help soften the pain, the typical widow, who may be unaccustomed to wealth, begins to buy things like a car, a different home, the massive renovation of "their" home, travels extensively to places "they" never visited or spends it on the charitable support of children, grandchildren or causes. Most of these decisions are designed to ease her emotional pain without considering the consequences to her own financial independence later.

Why is it people who have never had a large amount of money and then win a large lottery prize usually end up right back where they were financially, or sometimes worse? It is most likely that someone who has become a "self-made" millionaire has gone broke at least one or more times along the way. And yet, they seem to be able to make it all back.

The difference between the entrepreneur and the person who unexpectedly receives a large sum of money is *the poverty consciousness of spending.* Most new widows or lottery winners don't change their mindsets and find they can spend a million dollars just as easily as they could spend a thousand dollars in the past.

Entrepreneurs who get an idea, plan it, develop the clear vision of the outcome, create the methods of getting the vision realized and work very hard for its accomplishment, also have two huge factors working in their favor. First, a financially successful entrepreneur understands and appreciates what it took to earn the money in the first place. Second, the products or services created, the people they served and seeing their vision come to life, were the primary focus – not just the money.

When these factors come together successfully, another key realization kicks in for the entrepreneur; the entrepreneur *has the security* of knowing it can be recreated again and again.

One of the challenges that face the economies of most countries is the way families, culture and educational institutions program masses of young people into thinking they need to prepare for a "job" versus preparing for opportunities to serve others and thereby earn a living.

A common question adults often ask children is, "What do you want to be when you grow up?" It seems innocent enough, and usually produces interesting answers. But, it is the beginning of getting the child thinking he or she must choose an occupation or a job rather than the full range of their true possibilities. A question, alternatively phrased, might trigger the option of considering how they want to serve the world through finding their purpose, or remaining open to embrace the creative process of discovery. Is it that inquiring adults believe this is too heavy a concept to put to a child?

Well, maybe we don't give our children enough credit or the encouragement to explore other questions of creativity. Since the parent's vision of security is most often tied to having a job, the focus on the occupational job future for the child sets in motion a myth. The myth is there is security in a job. Of course, as long as someone has a job there may be security. But, as many millions discover over and over again, when the job market shrinks, security becomes elusive, both actually and psychologically.

Let's look at the design intent of a *job*. To begin with, it usually comes with a guaranteed base salary or wage per hour; the "floor". Then you are told you must stay within certain boundaries which fit your job description; the "walls". Next you come to understand that as long as you are in this specific job position you will probably not advance much higher in the organization; the "ceiling". When you put all three conditions of your job together (floors, walls, ceiling) you get a "box". With the box often comes the feeling of not really going anywhere.

There is certainly nothing wrong with being an employee with a job. It is what the life of most working people is all about. And, without dedicated workers doing their jobs, the economy would collapse. If, however, you lose the job and have to give up your box; or you just decide you don't want to do that particular job anymore; or you are retired and feeling the need to find more purpose and passion in your life by getting back into the world of the actively employed, it may be time to look for an opportunity that can change your financial outcome.

So now let's look at *opportunity*. First, and very important, there is no guaranteed "floor"! That means that within the pursuit of opportunity there is an *unlimited* opportunity to risk failure. Next, with a real opportunity there are no "walls" so there are no restrictive parameters that would limit the areas of opportunity to explore, including with whom, or how to pursue, anything. Finally, if you are successful, the design of a real opportunity should have no limits on your success, no "ceiling". This is the difference between *jobs* and *opportunities*.

Can you pursue opportunities within a job? Of course you can! There are many examples of this being possible. And, there are several factors required to be in place for this to occur:

a) Your willingness to continuously go "above and beyond" the minimum required just to keep your job.

b) Your willingness to innovate and add to the overall success of the organization as opposed to waiting for someone to somehow magically discover your extraordinary worth on their own just because you are employed there.

c) The structure and flexibility of your employer's organization.

d) Whether the organization is a small, closely or family held operation, or a large organization.

Any of these factors can play a significant role in your ability to find or create opportunity within your job.

As far as an entrepreneurial opportunity is concerned, there has never been a more perfect time for anyone, regardless of age, race, gender, background or training to start their own business than exists today. This may strike you as a bold statement, but the statement is founded on both what I have researched in the "new marketplace" of global connectivity and my personal acquaintance with start-ups.

One of the major reasons for this is that there has never been a time in recorded history that so much detailed information has been available to so many as in our current information age. There are very few subjects you might want to pursue that are not available at your fingertips, in your language, 24 hours a day, 365 days a year! And yet, amazingly, there is a growing trend of an attitude of scarcity and limitation as opposed to opportunity and abundance among people everywhere.

Also, I am living proof of what I write. Remember my own story in the Introduction of this book. Just one year ago I was wiped out financially. For most of us, this circumstance might trigger a feeling of being a failure. But there is something that is very important to learn about the word failure. *Failure is an event, not a person.*

My security comes from an internal knowing and confidence that opportunity is there for anyone. We simply need to choose to dedicate themselves to applying our lifetime of knowledge, skills and desire to a disciplined work ethic and a vision of how to use what we have to serve the betterment of others. As a result, I am living a life that I always dreamed of and saw in others. All of this has happened at a time when economic indicators and the news media are saying the general economy and the job market in the world today are about as challenging as they have been for several decades.

What about YOUR future?

Are you one of the 517 million Baby Boomers in the world facing decisions about retirement in the future? Or, maybe you have already retired. What are your options? If you are age 40, or older, you have something that is like gold you can mine to guarantee your financial future. This gold is also available to you regardless of what you may have ever done in the past.

The reason that I can make this statement with certainty is no one, and I really mean no one, seriously cares what you have done before. Sure, they may want to know about your "resume" as a formality. But, you and everyone else will be very interested in what you are *going* to do; what you are going to let spring from your creative being and how you are going to serve humanity in your own very unique way.

The gold you have to mine is as singularly unique as your finger print. It is that unique combination of wisdom, experience, vision, skills and perspective that will allow you to provide a service to others that no one else on the planet can do exactly like you.

You are one of a kind and when you harness those unique factors within you and you offer them up to serve your Human Family, as only you can, MAGIC happens! You get to find not only opportunity; you get to follow your "bliss". When that happens, you never have to work at a *job* for the rest of your life. This is because the ways you are serving others and how you spend your days is in harmony with your purpose in life. In return, you get to be in a state of fulfillment and financial abundance – a great place to live!

Look at the following list of these seemingly unrelated people and determine what two things they *all* have in common:

Agatha Christie	Voltaire
Oscar Hammerstein	Colonel Harland Sanders

Laura Ingalls Wilder
Joseph Baerman Strauss
Mother Teresa
Dr. William Mayo
Saint Augustine
Sophocles
Shirley McLain
Claude Monet
Cecil B. DeMille
Georgia O'Keeffe
Grandma Moses
Marc Chagall
Pope Gregory XIII
John Huston
Sigmund Freud
Eubie Blake
Michelangelo
George Bernard Shaw
Richard Wagner
Somerset Maugham
Daniel Chester French
Thomas Mann
Albert Einstein
Ethel Andrus
Thomas Jefferson
Euripides
Ben Franklin
Giuseppe Verdi
Barbara McClintock
Winston Churchill
Frank Lloyd Wright
James Michener

I could go on and on but this list is impressive enough. Have you guessed the two things they have in common? First, each started a business, launched a new work (as writer, artist, sculptor, etc.) or created an organization from scratch after the age of 60. Second, each one did it *without* the awesome global connectivity power of the Internet that you have available to you today!

If you are fully aware of the fact that business, as we know it to be, has now changed *forever* because of the Internet, ecommerce and social media, you immediately understand the significance of the second distinct advantage you have over all of the people on the list above. The explosion of opportunity through the connection to the global marketplace is not a spectator sport, however. You must get your ideas and services out on the World Wide Web!

You may have a lifetime of experience and, yet, you may feel you are underutilized and, as we say in Texas, feel like you have been "put out to pasture". If this is true for you, it may be time to reassess what you know and what you are truly passionate about, and get back in the game. In the world of Internet marketing, social media and global access, there is absolutely no reason not to participate.

Armed with your unique combination of experience, ideas, perspective, discipline, energy and, of course, a computer with connection to the Internet, you can start from scratch and build a business to serve people anywhere in the world within a relatively few short months. It is being done everyday. It doesn't have to be a multimillion dollar success story to significantly contribute to your life – and, the lives of others.

What would it take for you to be financially independent, by your definition? Unless you have already been living a lifestyle of the rich and famous and have the overhead expenses that go along with that lifestyle, chances are it can be achieved with a small business start-up today.

If you want to learn more about how to convert the gold that exists in your lifetime of knowledge, experience, skills and creativity into your own very real financial independence, I can highly recommend a resource that has served me incredibly well.

Just type expertsacademy.com into your browser. When you do, you will discover how you can take the gifts with which you were born, plus your lifetime of expertise and creative ideas, and share them with the world as never before.

I would not have written this book or launched RethinkAge.com without the Experts Academy and its founder, Brendon Burchard, as my resource and guide. This I know for certain from personal experience and observation, whatever you think is possible for you, you are probably underestimating it. So, if you have any curiosity about how you can positively influence the Financial Cord of your parachute by connecting what you have to offer to the world, check it out.

Brendon has proven one of his favorite sayings over and over again with people from literally every imaginable background. He says, "You can make a difference and a fortune sharing your advice". In today's world, there is no reason for you to not have the financial independence that you always dreamed of having!

Find your passion and take the first step!

CHAPTER 10
THE FUN CORD

"Isn't fun the best?"
A line from the 1981 film "Arthur"
- spoken by actor Dudley Moore.

Take a moment and open up your planning or appointment calendar. As you scan over what you have planned for the rest of this year, how many times you have specifically blocked out time for FUN? I have heard it said that if you have to think about having fun, you are "just not into it", and you have a problem. However, in the world of demands for the attention of the average adult, if you are *not* thinking about it, fun will most likely be gradually downgraded as a priority and pushed out of your regular experience. Most adults have succumbed to the more serious tasks and responsibilities that have taken over their lives since childhood when fun was a natural part of life.

There is an interesting dichotomy which develops in the typically responsible and task-oriented adult life. On one hand, all of the "adult stuff" tends to replace fun with stress. On the other hand, one of the absolute best ways to reduce stress is to have fun. Young children, as you know, do not carry the stress levels of most adults. Of course, children can emulate (or cause) stress with dramatic behavior at times. But this is not the same as the quietly debilitating stress many adults have allowed to build up over time.

So, how can you increase your childlike, stress-free fun and just enjoy life more? The first consideration I can offer comes from the flip side of the childlike fun behavior, which is boredom. You have surely observed no one can become bored as quickly, easily and more often as a child. My favorite response to the "I'm bored and there isn't anything to do" declaration of youth is the one you will recognize from a previous chapter:

The only way someone can be bored is in the absence of a good idea.

The same solution works for adults too. You may be someone who thinks, "I've got too much on my mind, agenda or whatever, to take the time to think about having fun". You may also have a self-image that you are just not a very fun person. What is more likely true is that the only thing standing between you and the development of the FUN Cord of your parachute is the amount of thought and attention you give to what would be fun for you. This may require you to carve out a bit of personal time for yourself, especially if you are in a routine that involves a close personal relationship with someone else.

Single people have less of an issue with this than those who are married or in a significant-other relationship. It is important to remember; however, those with whom you may live will find you much more energetic and fun to be with when you allow *fun* to be a larger part of your life. If they truly love you, they will even be happy for you! It nearly always warms the relationship with the ones to whom you are closest when they see the gleam of fun in your eyes. And, hey, they may even want to join in with you for their own fun.

Here are a few triggering thoughts that will help you create more fun in your life:

SMILE - Everyone knows that it takes a fraction of the facial muscles to smile than it takes to frown. Fortunately for us, smiling is simply a choice. Also, smiling is a choice that can quickly become a habit and that habit becomes your attitude and, eventually just who you *are*.

Once, Marilyn and I were driving over a mountain pass in Colorado when we decided to pull into one of those scenic spots to photograph the incredibly beautiful view. Another couple had pulled in near us and soon we were trading turns as each couple posed for photos with the range of valleys and mountains in the background. The man of the couple commented that Marilyn and I seemed like we were "made for each other" and explained that they had been dating for 6 years and were struggling with the decision whether or not to get married. He then turned to me and asked, "What is it about your wife that makes your marriage work for you?" Without even taking a breath, I looked and Marilyn and answered, "She wakes up smiling every day!" Then I turned back to him and said, "If you want to get married and make it work, you can wake up smiling everyday too."

How could you have a bad day when you choose to wake up smiling everyday? And don't forget – greater emotional well-being comes when you increase your SPH.

LAUGH OUT LOUD – No doubt you have heard the expression, "Laughter is the Best Medicine". This ancient proverb represents a deep truth for human beings in many ways. Laughter not only lifts the emotional mood and well-being in one's life, it also connects us with our highest spiritual self and swings open the gates of joy. An additional bonus is the positive effect laughter has on our physical health, as well.

Most oncologists will verify that a cancer patient's tendency to maintain a state of happiness and find every reason possible for humor and laughter has a dramatic impact on overcoming his or her physical challenges. In some cases such good spirits have the result of achieving wellness sooner and more completely.

Think about what makes you laugh out loud and throw yourself into those conditions. It is entirely possible to laugh your way to better health! Better yet, think about that baby's face that exploded with joy from discovering the *shiny object* in Chapter 4. What would it take for your face to explode with such joy? When you determine the answer – choose to do that!

MOVEMENT - In Chapter 4 we defined "a rut" as just a grave with both ends kicked out. The real quiet danger with ruts, though, is how quickly and easily we develop them. The neurotransmitters in the brain tend to associate a highly repeated activity (or lack of activity, such as sitting down and watching television for several hours every single day).

Through the process of association, the brain forms groups of like-neurons to create an emotional and physical comfort, of sorts, with the ability to turn most other neuron systems to their standby or off position. While relaxation is good, relaxing by repeatedly doing the same thing for long periods of time is not.

The quickest way to get a feeling of fun going for you in these moments is to get up and *move*! Movement of almost any kind is a terrific and simple "on" switch for the brain, and therefore, the rest of the nervous system and the body. A movement for you could be something as simple as walking around to the back or side of your chair and stretching or by recording that program you *must* watch while you take a walk around the block. Who knows? You may come across someone you haven't seen in a while and discover a fun conversation with a neighbor. Who needs a front porch after all?

GET OUTDOORS - It does not matter whether you think the weather outside its too hot or too cold, some of the least expensive and greatest sources of fun are in getting up and getting outside. Modern societies in developed nations have become spoiled to the habit and routine of maintaining both a comfort zone of activity and a comfort zone of temperature indoors.

Most people can't wait to get inside where the climate is determined by a thermostat on the wall. When was the last time you walked to a park, climbed onto a swing and discovered how high you could go? When was the last time you went to a nature trail and simply experienced why it is called that? When was the last time you had a contest with someone about the number of times you could skip a flat rock across a body of water?

The world outside holds much more creative promise for fun than the world inside will ever have. Why not go out and rediscover what outdoors means for the fun you can create for yourself and those whom you care about most?

SING AND DANCE - When Marilyn and I were on a Rotary International mission trip to Malawi and Zambia, in sub-Saharan Africa, we were reminded again and again of how much cost-free fun people can have just by getting on their feet and singing and dancing.

In the harsh shadow of some of the most poverty-bound parts of the planet, people of all ages were some of the happiest people we have met in any part of the globe. These beautiful people understood happiness was theirs to choose and how they had fun was available to each one every time they got up to sing and dance. They sang and danced to greet us. They sang and danced to share entertainment with us. We suddenly found our ourselves singing and dancing with them. Then they sang and danced to say goodbye.

There is a huge lesson in this natural habit of those happy people from which those of us more "civilized" members of our Human Family could benefit greatly. And, we could add a lot to fun to our lives in the process.

TIME WITH KIDS - If you don't have the remarkable energy, unconditional fun and joy of children in your life, in some form or another, it may be time to correct this missing piece. If you have kids or grandkids, or nieces or nephews in your family stop right now and create a plan for when and where you will make a regular connection with them, even if it is by phone or Skype.

If you don't have kids or grandkids, or nieces or nephews of your own, then find and choose a creative way that you can connect with some. For example, volunteering with Boys & Girls Clubs, Boy Scouts and Girl Scouts, various homes for children, adoption awareness movements, reading and mentoring programs in school, or any other plans to serve children.

You can choose to create endless opportunities to connect and have fun with children.

You may be only a short background check away from a opportunity to serve in a way that will keep you in the challenging and fun world of kids for many years to come. There is no possible way to measure the joy and fun, as well as positive influence, a decision like this could mean for the kids – and for you.

MUSIC - I remember the freedom I felt in my first car with an 8-Track tape player. I could play the music I wanted to select without have to have a record player to do it. Then, in the blink of a technological eye, we went from that to cassette tapes, CD's, and on to the explosion of digital music and other recordings.

Today, music of any variety and quality is at the fingertips of just about everyone on the planet. Don't worry about what those people driving along beside you are thinking as you are throwing yourself into that fun song you are singing along with so "perfectly". You don't care what they think anyway, right? So let yourself go and just have fun with it – (safely, of course)!

SPORTS - What is more fun than watching your favorite sport on television? *Playing a sport*! Yeah, that's the ticket!

You say you don't know how? You're too old? No way!

You can now learn almost any sport in the world and at any age. And, as far as age is concerned in sports, there is almost no sport in the world that doesn't have an Octogenarian Club associated with it.

I recently heard of a winner last year of a downhill slalom race who was over one hundred years of age. The lists of octogenarian bicyclist, swimmers, golfers, runners, softball players, tennis and racquetball players, bowlers, and scuba divers are plentiful. So what will your sport be? When was the last time you got up off the couch and felt the exhilaration and FUN of your favorite sporting activity? Maybe it's time for you to either revisit the sport that used to get your juices flowing or discover the thrill and fun of learning something completely new. Either way, it will put you in motion toward some of the fun that may have been missing in your life!

TURN FEAR INTO FUN – I have to admit, when I was about to load myself up in an airplane with three strangers intending to jump out of it 30 minutes later, there was some fear in my being. The pilot, videographer and jump-master who was clipped to my back were reassuring as we talked and joked our way through the climb to 10,500 feet above sea level.

Then they opened the door.

At that altitude it seemed weird and unnatural to a pilot such as me to experience this. But, then the moves to get into proper position and do my part to prepare took my total concentration. There simply wasn't time to be afraid.

Before I could think twice about what was going to happen next, we were in free fall for about 5,000 exhilarating feet. What an experience!

Within five seconds of leaving the plane, the videographer showed up in front of me giving me a *thumbs up*. We got close enough to give each other a high-five and any fears that I had were gone. At this point, there was only the fun and thrill of enjoying the amazing scenery and ride.

I am not recommending that you have to jump out of an airplane, or any other such experience, to have fun. But, I encourage you to take a hard introspective look at something that you have *wanted* to do, but fear has held you back. If you truly can't get it out of your mind, maybe it's time to explore what it would take to turn your fears into fun.

EXPLORE YOUR CREATIVITY - Dusting off that idea you have always wanted to explore and bringing fruition to it can be a great way to create fun. It doesn't have to be in the arts, literature or crafts that ignite your creative spark. John Dillon, author and public radio host wrote a fun and stimulating book entitled *The 20-20 Creativity Solution*. The book reminds those of us who have spent our entire lives in serious adult pursuits that there is a mountain of fun available to each of us that is just a thought away. As you might expect, John's book provides a unique perspective on the subject of creativity. You can learn more about it at the2020book.com.

DISCOVERY - There is an indigenous tribe of Havasupai Indians who live on a reservation in their native tributary of the Grand Canyon. In 1980, I had the privilege of hiking the Havasupai Trail to their village, to the Havasu Falls and the turquoise colored Mooney Falls.

Even after the passage of decades since that experience, I vividly remember what an amazing and sensorially delicious experience it was. The sight of the rainbow of the various red and yellow narrow canyon walls that rose up like skyscrapers above the trail and the unexpected and gorgeous plant life in the desert are visions I will never forget.

I even smile when I think about how much better the food seemed to taste when cooked down on the pristine canyon floor. There was no trash anywhere because when my hiking buddies and I checked in with the tribe, they told us the absolute rule that everything carried in had to be carried out.

Visitors were encouraged to leave only their footprints and admiration of the unique beauty of this "Garden of Eden" of the desert. The Havasu and Mooney Falls are some of the most beautiful I have ever seen – and I have seen falls in many parts of the world! I chose this experience to share the fun discovery adventure with you because this place is so tiny and isolated, and represents just one microscopic spec on this stunning home we all share called Earth. What would you like to discover – just for fun?

"FUN BUCKET LIST"

You have probably heard of the idea of creating a Bucket List. If for some reason you are not familiar with the term, it is a list of things you commit to do before you "Kick the Bucket", an American expression for dying.

I am suggesting that you refine the term to a "FUN Bucket List". As you have gathered by now, Marilyn and I have been very fortunate to travel and see a good bit of the world, and we look forward to seeing even more. However, if your Bucket List is just about the places you have not seen, it could turn out to be less than satisfying or fun. How many statues or cathedrals do you want to see in your lifetime? By adding the word "FUN" to the qualification for your bucket list, you challenge yourself to make the experience more truly remarkable and memorable. One additional element of adding fun to your Bucket List is to think about with whom you want to share the experience.

So, now it's your turn. Here is your moment to actually take some quality time and create your FUN Bucket List. When you have completed at least a minimum target of ten items on your list, go back and put your most critical "Fun Filter" on each. This is to test and make sure that how you will *feel* and what you will say when you imagine the accomplishment of each item. The test is to make the experience one that will make you exclaim, with feeling, "Wow, that was really fun!"

Go ahead and make your list now. I will be waiting for you in the NEXT chapter.

CHAPTER 11
THE RIP CORD

"There is no passion to be found in playing small - in settling for a life that is less than what you are capable of living."

- Nelson Mandela

Remember when I asked you in Chapter 2 to visualize the classic parachute design with the "D" shaped metal ring on the rip cord? As you reflect on and choose how you might apply the concepts from this book, think of the "D" shape of the rip cord D-ring as a symbol for your Desire. For when you choose to reach up and pull it, you release *all* the cords of your parachute.

What unfolds with that release of the canopy is your ability and will to create Desire for what you wish to fulfill in your lifetime. This Desire is what distinguishes you *as a human being*. When, and how often, you pull the rip cord D-ring also represents your ability and willingness to unleash your Desires to *employ all cords*, and meaning in your life; that distinguishes *you* among human beings.

You have probably noticed that the majority of people who have reached the upper limits of their age have experienced their world shrinking over a period of time. By shrinking, I mean their daily movements, involvement in their communities and interactions with others are dramatically curtailed compared to their previously more active life. For some, their world may have shrunk as a result of a significant medical event which restricts them physically. For most, however, their shrinking world is a result of the accumulation of their lifestyle choices from their younger days. That younger person of yesterday may be the *you* of today. The shrinking can begin with those seemingly innocent and tiny decisions to simply not move about on a regular basis. It can also begin with any other habits of thought that create a mostly sedentary lifestyle.

For most of us, this shrinking of our world will begin only if we do not consciously reject the status quo and also reject finding comfort in our ruts. As we have discussed, there is even a contributing anatomical factor in this process. Clustering and associating of like-neuron activity in our brains is formed when we practice the same routine over and over again. Each of us is at risk of attracting this fate unless we specifically choose to avoid it. We can do so by maintaining our awareness of the daily choices which will bring a sense of aliveness and fulfillment into our everyday experience.

Within the chapters of this book I have offered detailed resources and information about how all of this works in each major "Cord" of our human parachute. When you begin to progressively put it all together, you will discover that you will be living on the fast track to achieving your heart's desire.

Best selling author, Wendy Lipton-Dibner, recently wrote a book entitled *Shatter Your Speed Limits*. I can highly recommend her book and, when you read it, I believe that you will further discover how to not settle for a feeling of being stuck in any area of your life.

Wendy asks her readers a very compelling question which is, "If you woke up tomorrow morning and magically found you had everything you truly wanted, how would your life be different"? This question is worthy of your thoughtful consideration. It is the beginning point of finding the fuel for your Desires. (You can buy *Shatter Your Speed Limits* in the store at <u>shatteryourspeedlimits.com</u>.)

An emphasis on your great gift of the power of choice of what you feed your spirit, your mind and body has been repeated. However, I fully recognize and admit how puny the ideas and words are when they are just in print.

Your choice to find something of value within this book, and then to create your own decision to fire up your Desire to take specific action, will determine the relevance and value of this book and the time you have invested in reading it. So the fact that this book was even written, published, purchased and read, pales in comparison to what you choose to do with it!

Over many thousands of years, humans have tried to figure out ways to take their worldly possessions with them into the afterlife. As far as anyone can tell, any of these schemes have been an unsuccessful exercise. When people have an entire lifetime in a state of equating their own worth and self-image with their possessions, it is understandable they would want to believe they should be able to find some magical way to never have to give them up. As long as they have the stuff, the money, the job, the title, and the trappings of their egos, they feel empowered. So it is natural, from an egotistical perspective, to want to take their "power" with them.

And yet, Andrew Carnegie, who at one time was one of the wealthiest men in history, has been credited with saying, *"There is no class so pitiably wretched as that which possesses money and nothing else."*

This is a powerful statement from a real authority, given his philanthropic impact on his Human Family. It highlights the meaning of our need as humans to focus on our referral to the divine spirit that is within each of us. This is a truer and more permanently empowering point of reference which comes from within. It is brought out by finding your own path to the service of others. And, you don't have to have Carnegie's financial resources to live it out in your life.

By the simple acts of connecting with your Human Family; finding the courage and Desire to risk taking action; living your life full-throttle with movement and joy at every opportunity, you can find the significance that is your birthright. In fact, you can find more fulfillment in your life, while avoiding what I call the "Epitaph of Someone".

On the tombstone of "Someone Average", who does not have the cords of his parachute fully packed, his epitaph might read like this:

Here Lies "Someone Average"

Someone was born into an average family;

He lived an average life, never trying to excel at much of anything.

He tried hard to not accomplish much, and succeeded every time.

Someone worked at simply getting through life without too much discredit.

He never failed at any particular task because he never risked much.

So, here lies Someone Average;

Died at age 30,

Buried at age 80!

Instead, what I hope you have found, or rediscovered, in this book is what an incredibly blessed creature you are just by being uniquely you. You can use your power of choice to create your own fulfillment. You can choose to develop all of your unique gifts. Then you can choose to find your own creative ways to serve others by sharing your unique gifts and talents.

I once had the opportunity to watch a one-man play about the many, and somewhat radical, lectures by the, previously referenced, professor William James. The portrayal of James was reinforced by the fact that the actor was also a university professor and an avid James researcher.

He recreated one of James' lectures where he declared, "I have found the solution to all of the problems of mankind. All we have to do is to insist, from this day forward, that when each new baby is born, we pull them out and inform them, You are here to serve. If you have a different idea you are going back"!

Obviously this was an allegorical remark intended to shock and surprise his audience into thinking about the consequences of such a philosophy. Although it was a radically strange way of saying it, there is a powerful truth within its meaning and intent. If each and everyone born on our planet knew, embraced and acted out the belief that they are here to serve others, what an amazingly wonderful world we might have in the future.

When Marilyn's father, "Pop" as he was known to the family, was still alive, I was fortunate to have benefitted from a few gems of wisdom he shared with me. One of those gems had to do with a dilemma I discovered I had with the motto of Rotary International, when I was as a new member. The motto is "*Service Above Self*".

I had to confess to Pop, who was a seasoned Rotary member and officer, that I was struggling with this concept. The reason was my discovery that every time I served someone else, I felt I got more out of the act of serving others *for* myself than I was delivering. "So how are the consistent benefits I feel within myself not in conflict with the motto?" I asked. Pop simply stated, with his typical economy of words, "It is about your intention".

I understood both his words and his assuring tone immediately. When any one of us goes into an act of service for others with the pure intention of serving their benefit alone and not intending or anticipating any gain or benefit for ourselves, it sets up one of the greatest flows of spiritual energy that can transpire between human beings. This is what I now call "spiritual affluence". The outcome of that intention is almost always what you will recognize as what's called a "win - win situation." Remember what was shared with you in Chapter 4 about intention and then combine it with this idea:

**When it comes to the spiritual affluence of serving others,
it is not a question of you doing everything,
but it is a question of you doing something!**

Take some quality time to think about it and you absolutely know your own heart's Desire. Risk letting that Desire loose by pulling your own rip cord "D-ring" to what's NEXT in your life. Whatever that decision may be, you can rely on the strengthening you have done on the many "Cords", the Spiritual, Mental, Physical, Vital Health, Emotional, Relationships, Financial and FUN cords of your parachute, to get you where you want to go.

The moment you realize you have fine-tuned these mutually beneficial cords of your parachute, pulling the rip cord on the daily opportunities to live an extraordinary life will be something to which you look forward to every day. You will discover that living your life in a constant state of *thrival* is much, much better than living your life in a state of *survival* and just getting by each day, no matter how much money you have.

In Chapter 3, we discussed that the only thing absolutely guaranteed for each of us is we won't get out of this life alive. Since none of us knows when the end will come, it is important we balance, square up and pack our own parachute to the highest standard possible for the *flight of our lives* with what matters most to us each and every day. Wouldn't it be a transcendent feeling to know, for certain, when you have come to the end of your life, through one successful life parachute jump after another, you can honestly know the unedited truth within your heart and say:

**I lived life fully,
I loved deeply at every chance,
I took every opportunity to put on a smile and dance,
I made a difference serving my Human Family;
and, wow, I finished my life skidding in sideways saying,
"*What a ride*"!**

I wish for you an extraordinary ride from this day forward!

ACKNOWLEDGEMENTS

This book was written with great joy in my heart, deep gratitude and acknowledgement of the influences that have made the writing possible. First are my parents, C.F. and June from a medium-sized town in the middle of West Texas with a huge tradition of solid common-sense values. Their values were born and shaped from their faith in God and their belief we are all here to serve and help each other.

My parents were influenced by growing up in the Great Depression of the 1930's and the impact of World War II on their lives as young adults and newlyweds. Their devotion to God and Country was a natural part of their lives. Their encouragement and belief in me, as I grew up without the hardships that were such a big part of their childhood and young adulthood, was laced with unconditional love and the constant message I could do anything I set my mind to do. This is an incredibly powerful gift any parent, or grandparent, can give a child.

When I was still an infant, my mother drove me across the country by herself, from one Army

Air Corps training base to another as my dad developed his skills to survive as a tail-gunner on a B-25 bomber in North Africa, the Mediterranean and over Italy during World War II.

I often reflect back on her stories of rationing, little money and her even having to stop in the middle of a cross-country trip to ask a farmer for milk from one of his cows to give to me. It makes perfect sense that any improvements they were able to build in their lives afterward, made it easy for them to see a world of better possibilities for me and my younger brother, Keith.

Then there were friends, pastors, Scoutmasters, fellow Boy Scouts and Eagle Scouts, band directors, teachers, baseball and track coaches, U.S. Army drill sergeants, commanders and my comrades in arms, college professors, employers, business partners, employees, customers, clients and my many close friends and acquaintances who have each taught me powerful and wonderful lessons.

The experience of being married, more than once, having three amazing children and five beautiful grandchildren has added to the joy and fulfillment that I have found with my wife of 28 years, Marilyn. And my gratitude for Marilyn is as undying and unconditional as the unconditional love, faith and support that she has always provided to me. They have all taught me that there are many different ways to live and love. These are the things for which I am most grateful.

My gratitude also goes out to the countless teachers, speakers, authors, seminar leaders, video and audio producers and other centers of insight and influence who have had the courage to show me the way along my journey in this life. These pioneers who have put their fears, doubts and worries aside and given full flight to their messages are real heroes for which I am deeply grateful. They have shown me that the faith and courage to act on my passion to serve God by serving my Human Family (that would include you) is not only possible, but that it *must be shared* to have meaning.

Just like you, I have experienced many challenges in my journey but, I also revel in the lessons learned from those challenges. One of my favorite quotes is, "the same hammer that shatters glass, also forges steel". I am so very grateful I have been taught that I can choose how each of the hammer blows will improve my life.

And, now I encourage you to find your voice and do the same for others.

ABOUT THE AUTHOR

Dave McSpadden is a speaker, author, trainer, seminar leader and the founder and CEO of RethinkAge Institute, and RethinkAge.com.

Born and raised in San Angelo, Texas, his model of serving others was learned from his parents and experiences in Scouting where he earned both the God and Country Award and the rank of Eagle Scout. After graduating from high school and a tour in the U.S. Army, he attended San Angelo College, majoring in Business. Dave had a 40-year career in commercial construction, the last 26 of those years as President and C.E.O. of his own company.

Since joining the Rotary Club of Waxahachie (Texas) in November 1984, he has served his Club, Rotary International and his community in many leadership roles. Dave is honored to have served the North Central Texas Clubs of Rotary International District 5810 as District Governor in the Rotary Year 2009-10 and he is an Assistant Regional Coordinator for Rotary International, serving Rotary Districts in Texas and Oklahoma.

Dave is a graduate of Life Mastery University, consisting of five different courses by Tony Robbins between 2001 and 2005, which culminated with the final Life Mastery course at Tony's resort in Fiji.

At RethinkAge Institute, Dave is committed to helping people create life choices toward peak performance at any age by finding more creative purpose, productivity and passion in their lives. He has spoken to thousands about using their "power of choice" to realize their full personal potential.

He and his wife and business partner, Marilyn, were married on a mountaintop in Vail, Colorado in 1983. They are grateful for their three happily married children and five grandchildren.

Feeling blessed for all of their opportunities to serve their Human Family in the world, Marilyn and Dave are honored to have had the chance to be involved in numerous Rotary International mission trips and projects. These include multiple wheelchair distributions in Mexico which have provided mobility to hundreds of recipients. They are also grateful for having been privileged to work on improving a primary school, providing secondary student scholarships, safe water and sanitation projects in Malawi, Africa and safe water wells in Zambia, Africa.

Dave believes his purpose on this earth is to serve God by serving mankind. It is his fervent hope that by sharing this book with you that he has assisted you in continuing to define your purpose, as well.

Dave is donating a portion of each book purchased to The Rotary Foundation of Rotary International and would like to thank you for your support.

www.ingramcontent.com/pod-product-compliance
Lightning Source LLC
Chambersburg PA
CBHW061259110426
42742CB00012BA/1984